One life at a time

Children's Home
news

Winter 1987-88

THIS ISSUE

Thursday's Child

One life at a time

Children's Home Society of Minnesota

1889-1989

Kenneth L. Green

Children's Home Society of Minnesota • St. Paul • 1989

Project manager: Mary Ann Nord
Cover illustration: Linda Frichtel
Cover design: Judy Savage/PDR
Text design, production editor: Ellen B. Green
Indexing: Suzanna Moody
Printer: Sexton Printing, Inc.

All photos and illustrations are from the archives of Children's Home
Society of Minnesota except as follows: Photos on pages 9-10, 15, and 19-
22 are from the collections of the Minnesota Historical Society and are
reproduced with permission. Other photos were supplied by: pages 11, 14
Dorothy Pippert Halupnik; page 38 Sally Onan Healey; page 46 *St. Paul
Pioneer Press Dispatch;* page 47 Alexander G. Hill; page 53 Meg Bale.

Contents

Preface

This story celebrates the hundredth birthday of Children's Home Society of Minnesota as a premier provider of quality social services for children and families. Words like *pioneering, innovative,* and *caring* have come to define the society through the work of the five men profiled here. Along with many thousands of others, they gave their money, time, talents, and hearts for the benefit of children. They did so in different settings, in different times, in response to differing specific needs, and with different resources. They interceded in many ways, with many hours, many dollars, and many kindnesses in many children's lives, but each worked thoughtfully, with just one child at a time.

To sociologists or historians, the groups of children on the Orphan Train, in the Receiving Home, the Lincoln House, and the day care centers are interesting, perhaps even compelling. But in each face the caseworkers and volunteers of Children's Home Society have seen just one child, needing the care and support of a loving family to reach full potential. For most of a century that meant finding a home. Today, it means much more—child care, family and individual counseling, pregnancy counseling, the prevention of child abuse—whatever services might help make families work better.

The society's newsletter, *Children's Home Finder* (later *Children's Home News*), provided valuable information for this book. Much early detail comes from Savage's notes and from LeRoy Ashby's book, *Saving the Waifs: Reformers and Dependent Children, 1890-1917* (Philadelphia: Temple University Press, 1984). Other sources include unpublished manuscripts, "History of the Children's Home Society of Minnesota, 1889-1927" by the Reverend S. W. Dickinson, "Fifty Years of Child Care: Children's Home Society of Minnesota, 1889-1939" by Esther Levin, and "The Children's Home Society of Minnesota, 1937-1980" by John Hueg (1981); annual meeting addresses, "Early History of the Children's Home Society" by George V. Thomson (1958) and "Two Decades of Adoption—and After" by Charles B. Olds (1967); board minutes; recollections; interviews; and miscellaneous documents in the society's possession.

This small book is the result of many hands, especially those of the Centennial History Subcommittee: board members Eleanor J. Andersen and Drexel Van Every, staffers Barbara Crandall, Mary Scanlan, Lon Berg, ZoeAnn Wignall, Mary Muelken, and Mary Ann Nord. Volunteer Marj Meyer was generous in sharing her previous research. Many reviewed the manuscript and contributed personal stories. Jack Foley and Sexton Printing, Inc., donated part of the manufacturing costs, John Wickre donated type scanning services, and Suzanna Moody donated the indexing. Finally we thank marketing specialist Peter D. Reese for simple words providing a theme to celebrate the tradition of Children's Home Society of Minnesota:

> Well, it's a never-ending story:
> Children with important needs
> Waiting for someone to care—
> Tiny voices, silent pleas.
>
> We change so very many lives
> When we open up our minds
> And know we can really help, right now—
> One child, one home, one life at a time.

—KENNETH L. AND ELLEN B. GREEN
Adoptive parents and co-chairs
Centennial History Subcommittee

The

HOME FINDER

Organ of

The Children's Home Society

. . . of Minnesota . . .

VOL. V. No. 2	MAY, 1904	25 cents per year

PUBLISHED QUARTERLY BY THE
CHILDREN'S HOME SOCIETY OF MINNESOTA
Jean Martin Brown Receiving Home, 2239 Commonwealth Ave.,
St. Anthony Park, St. Paul, Minn.

1 *Homes with a little "h"*

The Reverend Edward P. Savage, founder of Children's Home Society of Minnesota and its publication, the Home Finder.

Children's Home Society of Minnesota was quick to embrace the idea of child placing—matching orphans and neglected children with families—and quick to expand on it, pointing the way to modern child welfare practices.

The Reverend Edward Payson Savage, founder of the society, was a Baptist minister who first heard of child placing from Martin Van Buren Van Arsdale, founder of the national home society movement. Savage was deeply moved by a speech Van Arsdale gave in 1886 in Clinton, Iowa. To him, the idea of finding each child a family instead of caring for children in orphanages was "so sensible, so natural, so in accordance with the divine plan that it took hold of my convictions as a true way to care for homeless children."

Though Savage was to become a pivotal figure in the home society movement, he was at first an obscure preacher in St. Paul, and despite his enthusiasm, Van Arsdale and his associates advised Savage against trying to organize a home society in Minnesota. They suggested he form a local advisory board in St. Paul instead. Savage, however, felt the "greatness of the work" that child placing was about. With vision and energy, he began in June 1889 to "seek out homeless and grossly neglected children . . . [and] place the same in good homes by adoption or otherwise."

Accompanied by fellow St. Paul clergyman J. P. Dysart, Savage visited ministers and leading citizens in St. Paul, Minneapolis, and Stillwater, then Anoka, Champlin, Mankato, Kasota, St. Peter, Winona, Red Wing, Faribault, and Duluth. He located four needy children in the summer of 1889, placing one of them with a family. With the other three children waiting for homes, he and Dysart received six more applications for "certain children" from local groups forming in the communities they had visited. Twelve families assured the two ministers they were ready to receive a child, and thirteen more families were considering it.

After the well-known and beloved president of the University of Minnesota, Dr. Cyrus Northrop, agreed to serve as the first president of the board of directors, Savage called a meeting for September 11, 1889, to organize the Children's Aid Society of Minnesota as an "undenominational organization for the statewide care of homeless children by placing them in Christian homes." Selecting Northrop and convincing him to serve was a stroke of genius on Savage's part, for according to Minnesota historian Theodore C. Blegen, the scholar was "urbane, wise, witty, kindly, and patriarchal . . . a master of mellow and persuasive oratory" who "endeared himself to the people [and] won support from every group." Van Arsdale attended the organizational meeting in Minneapolis, urging the new society to affiliate with the national association of children's home societies.

With Savage as superintendent and Dysart as financial secretary, the Children's Aid Society began its work in Minnesota, northern Wisconsin, and the Dakotas. One of Savage's first tasks was to establish a firm legal footing for placing children. Minnesota laws regarding dependent and neglected children—like those of most other states—were not uniform. In fact, the idea that government bore anything beyond the barest responsibility for such children was not well accepted. "We do not consider that it is the province of the State to bring up [homeless] children, but simply to take charge of them temporarily," Dr. Hastings Hart of the Minnesota State Board of Charities and Corrections proclaimed in 1889. After considerable lobbying by Savage and others, the Minnesota legislature accepted the recommendations of the society in 1893, enacting a law "relating to the Societies organized for the purpose of securing homes for orphans." This gave the society's work legal status for the first time, placing it under the supervision of the ten-year-old State Board of Charities and Corrections.

Savage, a tireless worker, handled many of the society's early placements himself, gathering and delivering children and checking on earlier placements. In the year beginning September 1890, he traveled nearly 25,000 miles by horse and wagon, slow local trains, streetcars, and on foot. There was always more to do for the children, and his other responsibilities included fundraising, publicity, lobbying, appearing in court on behalf of neglected children, and editing the *Home Finder*.

His wife, Kate Snoad Savage, who ran the society's Minneapolis office, was also very busy. She was especially adept at raising money and gaining the attention of powerful and influential people, among them F. H. Peavey, the Pillsburys, and Captain John Martin, a railroad executive. In a single three-month period in 1891, she wrote over a thousand letters and traveled 1,500 miles on behalf of the society. Economic adversities and natural disasters often made her job harder. At the annual meeting of 1895, for example, the Reverend Savage reported that the great Hinckley Fire and other fires in Minnesota that year, as well as cyclones, had "rendered it very difficult to collect funds, not only in the regions thus suffering but in other places that responded to their appeals for aid."

A year earlier, at the request of the National Conference of Charities and Corrections, Savage had studied the "gigantic evil" of child desertion and estimated the number of deserted children in the country was at least 60,000 and might be more than 200,000. Desertion was not against the law in nine of thirty states, and even the states that did have child-desertion laws seldom enforced them. Savage influenced Minnesota legislation that (for a while, at least) treated desertion as a felony rather than as a misdemeanor.

Despite his wish to find homes for as many of the children as possible, Savage had high standards. Applicants for children, he told the Minnesota State Conference of Charities and Corrections in 1895:

Kate Snoad Savage, shown upon her fiftieth wedding anniversary, introduced the society to endowment funds. The first $20,000 came from several individual contributors including "Empire Builder" James J. Hill of St. Paul, and the Minnetonka Mill Company, makers of Nature's Breakfast Food. Contributions between 1903 and 1911 eventually pushed the initial endowment to $70,000, which provided income until it was depleted during the Great Depression.

Aboard the Orphan Train

The notion of child placing started with nineteenth-century reformer Charles Loring Brace, originator of the famous "Orphan Train." Brace founded the New York Children's Aid Society in 1853, which among other efforts and organizations gathered homeless and disadvantaged children from the streets of East Coast cities and sent them west in search of homes. Many of the children were orphans whose immigrant parents had died en route to or soon after arriving in America.

"Mr. Matthews set the children, one by one, before the company, and in his stentorian voice gave a brief account of each," wrote an eyewitness to one Minnesota stop of the train. Dr. Hastings Hart, a contemporary of E. P. Savage and chairman of the Minnesota State Board of Charities and Corrections, said:

> Applicants for children were then admitted in order behind the railing and rapidly made their selection. Then, if the child gave assent, the bargain was concluded on the spot. It was a pathetic sight, not soon to be forgotten, to see those children, tired young people, weary, travel-strained, confused by the excitement and the unwanted surroundings, peering into those strange faces, and trying to choose wisely for themselves . . . In a little more than three hours nearly all those forty children were disposed of.

Between 1854 and 1929 at least a hundred thousand and perhaps half again that many youngsters were put aboard the Orphan Train, said to have been the greatest mass movement of children since the Children's Crusade of the thirteenth century. The New York Children's Aid Society alone sent west at least 25,000 children; one was Benjamin Morris Pippert.

Only eighteen months old, Ben was the youngest of five Brooklyn siblings whose stepmother had rejected them. When the five arrived at the tiny Iowa farming community of Dysart in 1894, they were put up on a platform for display—a common practice leaving us with the expression "put up for adoption." They and other children on the Orphan Train had traveled from New York in a lice-infested boxcar, eating nothing but bread kept in a clothes basket. Ben wore a tiny velveteen coat with a pinned-on card giving his name and birthdate, November 12, 1892. He had nothing else.

Reciting a story probably oft-repeated in the Pippert household, Ben told how he had spied a mustached man resem-

Mina and Ben Pippert

bling his father. "Dada!" the toddler cried. The man picked him up, announcing, "I'll take this little fella home." The man was Henry Pippert, a grocery store clerk whose wife was expecting their first child. "Imagine what [she] said when he got home!" Pippert mused at a gathering of Orphan Train travelers at Children's Home Society in 1981.

Ben grew up as the older brother of Mina, and he did not learn that he was not part of the Pippert family by birth until he was eleven or twelve. One day, after helping a neighbor plow corn, he came home to find a man sitting on the porch with his father. "I am your real father," the stranger said as he reached out to touch Ben. "No, you're not!" the startled boy cried, retreating to Henry's arms.

Charles Morris had come from New York to reclaim his five children, all of whom had been placed with Dysart families. "You will never take him out of this town," Henry Pippert told him. "He will stay right where he is and he will carry the Pippert name as long as he lives." Morris remained in Dysart for four days, then, accepting the situation, returned alone to New York, where he died the following year.

As Henry Pippert had vowed, Ben Pippert never left Dysart. He opened a dray line when he was nineteen, sold it two years later, and with the profits bought a farm and got married in 1914. "My father's life proved to be a hard but a good life," wrote his daughter, Dorothy Pippert Halupnik, in October 1981. "Mom and Dad farmed for forty-seven years. They raised six children, and never forgot to thank God each day."

must be well approved as being kind-hearted, humane, mentally competent, Sabbath observing and church going, as it is the aim of the Society to place them in Christian families. They must also be strictly temperate and worthy of confidence for their honesty, morality, and trustworthiness. They must be in such financial circumstances as to give the child good advantages of education.

But as a former minister, Savage felt capable of assessing people personally, and he did not keep detailed records or make in-depth preplacement investigations. In fact, 1895 was the first year the society's placement application asked for even the occupation, income, and references of prospective caregivers.

In need of both more good homes and better funding, the society decided to enlarge its membership base at the suggestion of a writer whose letter appeared in the January 1896 *Children's Home Finder:*

> Any foster or adoptive parent should automatically become a member and anyone else who shall pay to the society each year the average cost to the society of taking, caring for & placing children which as I understand it is about $50. This will give to each member at each recurring Xmas the consciousness that during the previous year he has given a good home to one homeless child.

Edward Savage's hope to find a home for every child led him to write this 1907 diatribe against a stuffed toy popular during President Teddy Roosevelt's administration: "The Teddy bear is a bundle of fur skins shaped like a young bear and filled with excelsior or sawdust. And women cuddle these bundles on the street or fondle them at theaters. The thing is more childish than the lap dog habit . . . The woman who rejects her mission, who regards a child as an 'incumbrance,' and who tries to fill her arms and her heart with a rag and a hank of hair is . . . justly doomed—to bitterness of mind and soul. The Teddy bear fad is more than silly. It is a pathetic spectacle of perverted motherhood."

The confusing laws of this period failed to define child placement or "a good home." One group thought it meant indenture, a concept rooted in the laws of Elizabethan England. The society's first printed placement contracts were indenture agreements through which couples pledged to keep girls in their care until age sixteen, boys until age eighteen. Then they were to give the young adults "a new Bible and two complete new suits of neat and comfortable clothing," plus a sum of money (usually between fifty and a hundred dollars). Another school of thought was that placement meant finding permanent "foster" homes in which families cared for children without payment. Though many of these homes were otherwise the equivalent of today's adoptive homes, the children placed did not become legal members of their families. This was the primary approach of the society well into the twentieth century; probably fewer than one-fourth of pre-1920 Children's Home Society placements were legal adoptions.

While the experts argued over the best approach, the society had been working to extend the 1893 law that limited placement to children under the age of two. Unable to do so even by the time it changed its name to Children's Home Society of Minnesota at the May 1896 annual meeting, the society reincorporated the next year under an old law allowing it to gain custody of children under twenty-one if it became an orphan asylum. When the Minnesota legislature amended the 1893 law in 1899 to give placement societies legal guardianship to age ten, the society reverted to its original incorporation.

During the society's first years, Savage was able to place children almost immediately, but they soon began to outnumber prospective homes—nearly 1,100 children were in the society's care by 1897. Though many of these children were placed in homes, from one-fourth to one-half were eventually returned, and those requiring medical care or awaiting court hearings were boarded temporarily in scattered, private Twin Cities homes, greatly complicating more permanent arrangements. Some children reached the society's care near death, though Savage was proud of the agency's comparatively low death rate. He reported 4 percent of children in the society's care died in 1897, "while many institutions report losses of 35-70% among infants."

According to the January 1901 Children's Home Finder, *the society received many children in a week's time: "Tuesday brought a messenger from the western part of the state with five children, four sturdy little boys and a little girl all of one family . . . Wednesday two wee waifs, each with a story of suffering and sorrow very long for its brief life of a few weeks, were brought into the office . . . Then from distant Moorhead came a call to take the young babe of a mother deserted by her companion who must be relieved of the care of her baby that she might provide for her older child . . . The next day came a letter from a pastor at Buffalo, Minnesota, telling of a mother who had died this week leaving six children. The father has been able to provide for all but the month-old baby, and in his poverty and bereavement appealed to us."*

To Savage, "child-saving" was more than a poetic turn of phrase, and the death of a single child was too many. "Every child, well and wisely placed in a good home," he wrote in the October 1898 *Children's Home Finder* "is a living argument for the plan, and homes are opened for more children where at first it was difficult to find any." He wrote in November of the next year that the society had spent $74,000 in its first decade, caring for 1,450 "little ones . . . in the best way possible—by securing homes for them in kind and loving families."

So despite his strong belief in finding one home for each child, the steady flow of children led Savage to consider establishing a temporary "receiving" home for children awaiting placement. The society established its first such home at a private residence in Minneapolis in 1897, a second one "of sufficient size and centrally located" soon afterward in St. Paul, followed by a single combined facility at 463 Fairview Avenue in St. Paul. The number of children continued to increase, however, and some children were boarded elsewhere, posing such difficulties by the society's tenth anniversary that the board voted during a special meeting on July 5, 1899, to raise $10,000 for a larger home.

The plan to build ran into trouble almost immediately, when the state opposed the home on the grounds it might supplant the state school for the care of dependent children at Owatonna. Savage argued—successfully— that the state did not serve children of all ages, that many children required prompt attention, and that some children were deprived of care there because their parents did not wish to be branded as paupers.

Even with state acquiescence, however, the society could not break ground. There was no ground until October 19, 1900, when St. Paul philanthropist Joseph L. Elsinger deeded the society property in St. Anthony Park. He asked that a memorial tablet and a picture of his mother "be placed and always remain in the building." (Elsinger later joined the society's board, and his son Karl W. Elsinger succeeded him, serving twenty-two years.) Soon after Elsinger's unexpected gift, Kate Savage persuaded Captain Martin to underwrite the bulk of construction, which eventually totaled $40,000.

The pioneer founders of Children's Home Society of Minnesota were among the first to espouse the idea of children's rights. "The idea that the parent had absolute control of the life and the destiny of the child, that nothing short of some heinous crime should deprive him of his child, prevailed in all ages and still has its adherents even in our own age," Savage wrote in the *Home Finder* in 1901. He declared that the "supreme right of the child to be well brought up . . . transcends the right of the parent." His colleague, the Reverend D. B. Jackson, had proclaimed at the 1899 annual meeting that the society stood for child protection and "the highest possible estimate of the worth of the waif child."

Savage's idea of children's rights included means to a better life. The children in the care of the society, he wrote in a 1902 *Home Finder:*

> grow up with a well established acquaintance with the tools . . . of the family home—the washboard, the mop, the breadboard, the woodbox, yet wholesome things in their way, teaching self-help, self-reliance, independence. In the lives of these poor children, too often waifs of indolence and ignorance, these are the stepping stones of comfort and respectability, and [later] their chances for luxuries are good.

The society informed prospective families of its requirements for placement with cards like this.

TERMS ... WHICH BOYS ARE PLACED IN HOMES.

ALL APPLICANTS MUST BE ENDORSED BY THE COMMITTEE

Boys fifteen years old are expected to work till they are eighteen for their board and clothes. At the end of that time they are at liberty to make their own arrangements.

Boys between twelve and fifteen are expected to work for their board and clothes till they are eighteen, but must be sent to school a part of each year, after that it is expected that they receive wages.

Boys under twelve are expected to remain till they are eighteen, and must be treated by the applicants as one of their own children in matters of schooling, clothing and training.

Should a removal be necessary it can be arranged through the committee or by writing to the Agent.

The Society reserves the right of removing a boy at any time for just cause.

We desire to hear from every child twice a year.

All Expenses of Transportation are Paid by the Society.

CHILDREN'S AID SOCIETY.
24 ST. MARKS PLACE, N.Y.   E. TROTT, AGENT.

The Jean Martin Brown Receiving Home opened at the end of April 1903. Though the society intended it for use only as a temporary stop for children awaiting homes, many observers viewed it as an orphanage.

The dark red brick, three-story Jean Martin Brown Receiving Home that opened at the end of April 1903 would help achieve these ends. The building was named for Captain Martin's deceased daughter, whose son Earle Brown would become sheriff of Hennepin County and benefactor and board member of the society. The new building could accommodate fifty children—many fewer than the need—but it was thoroughly modern. It had some thirty rooms heated by steam, six large bathrooms, and a complete laundry. Over the portal the facility's name was engraved in letters of gold, and in the reception room was a marble bust of Elsinger's mother.

As the building went up, Savage continued his press for legislation in other states and tried to build a coalition in his own, emerging as a major national advocate of child welfare. At the annual convention of the National Children's Home Society in 1902, for example, he urged his colleagues to support laws regarding adoption, supervision of children placed in homes, and supervision of children placed in other states. But no one in the home society movement wanted government overly involved in child placement. W. B. Sherrard, superintendent of South Dakota's Children's Home Society, argued that private charity was preferable because human kindness—not

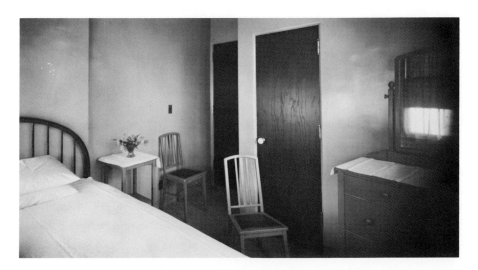

"Our new home is now complete and handsomely furnished," reported the November 1903 Home Finder. *"We are glad to have from the ladies of St. Anthony Park helpful suggestions in making the home pleasing and attractive."*

politics—guided the process. Still, widespread public acceptance of child placement in the state and elsewhere helped establish the legal standing of the home societies.

But the never-ending work of finding homes was exhausting. Worn out from trying to help every child in need, Savage wrote in 1903: "There is a limit to human endurance." He frequently witnessed suffering and abuse— three children covered with sores were abandoned to the streets, three others found their father in jail, and one infant was left cold and crying after his father had killed the mother, two relatives, and himself. Savage himself was occasionally threatened—by a drunken man who had badly mistreated his two children and again by a jailed woman who wanted to shoot him for taking her child. Once he rescued such children, Savage still faced the problem of finding them homes. Even then his job was not over. One woman returned a little girl after three months, saying, "I do not wish to keep her." Another family returned a boy: "He is not the boy we want." Some children died soon after being placed.

The May 1908 Home Finder *urged readers: "Come to the Home if the advice of one little girl applies in your case, when she said, 'Babies and grandmothers are nice to have in the house.' We can't furnish the grandmother, but we have lots of babies who need homes."*

Perhaps in reaction to criticism about such cases, Savage wrote in the *Home Finder* in February 1906:

> The children we place in homes are not perfect. Kindly remember that these children have had some sort of a home before, that they have formed associations, that their affections have been twined about other individuals. They are like the transplanted plant or tree . . . they are transplanted in your home.

Savage experienced happier moments, too. When he appealed to a St. Paul church congregation about a child no one seemed to want, for instance, a girl asked her mother, "Why can't we take that little boy?" They did, and the boy grew up to be a college professor.

Savage was an especially strong advocate of a belief basic to the home society movement—opposition to orphanages and other such asylums for homeless and neglected children. He wrote in the November 1904 *Home Finder* that, when the society was founded:

> the prevailing idea of the day [was] that in order to provide for homeless children a Home with a big "H" must be built first of all, overlooking the fact that God had thousands of homes spelled with a little "h" far preferable as a place for a homeless child to the best asylum ever built.

The society tried to establish its new receiving home as a temporary step toward individual placement by framing a new intake policy: It would accept only children who were then thought suitable for placement. This not only eliminated boarding but also served to turn away children with disabilities. Furthermore, the society would neither accept children to conceal "unlawful parentage" or "condone wrong-doing" nor take children whose parents simply no longer wanted to care for them. Later stating that "this institution is not a maternity hospital," the society also refused to take infants younger than three months old.

Although the need for receiving homes was evident at nearly all the state societies, they appeared to many observers to be just like the orphanages that the home society movement had opposed for two decades. "The receiving homes," said Dr. Hastings Hart (by this time superintendent of the National Children's Home Society) at the national convention in St. Paul in 1907, "are designed only for the temporary care of children . . . [although] in many cases the period of detention is somewhat extended." Children's Home Soci-

Monet girl
Minn
Aug 27-28

Dear mrs Tompson
I am writing and let yoy know
I like my new home best of all the home I have got many new cloths I will stur school next week thanks for the card how is my brother
with love from
clara

Described in the Home Finder *as "the stork of Minnesota," Ellen Thompson, an early society worker, wrote in January 1900: "I remember taking a little boy with me to church one Sabbath . . . I held that dear little fellow up before the people, asking someone to take him and give him a home and the training he so much needed. After the service was over, a man and his wife came to me and touched me on the shoulder and said, 'Mrs. Thompson, if I thought I could love that child as much as if it were born to me, I would be tempted to take it.' Immediately I laid the little fellow in his arms and said, 'The Lord only asks you to do the best you can.' " Another child she placed later wrote her the letter at left.*

ety of Minnesota was proud of its handsome and well-appointed Jean Martin Brown Receiving Home. But because some thought the facility was an orphanage, it raised complex social issues that may have contributed to a scandal involving the society on the eve of its twentieth anniversary.

Late in 1908, assistant superintendent A. H. Tebbets, a minister from Dawson, Minnesota, and two other society employees accused Savage of graft and corruption. Under Savage, Tebbets charged, the society had failed to check on children it had placed. It had, he said, handled its affairs with "generally unbusiness-like, unmethodical management," betrayed the Christian principles of its founding, and accepted illegitimate children, "thus making vice easy."

The board of directors began an immediate investigation, questioning Savage's effectiveness as an administrator but quickly declaring him innocent of graft. All of the society's funds could be accounted for and there was no evidence of misuse of money. The board found the other charges rested on philosophical differences between Savage and Tebbets over matters of policy. Although vindicating the founder, the directors realized the scandal had seriously threatened the society. They relieved both Savage and Tebbets of their administrative duties (Savage himself suggested it). Tebbets left the society, but Savage stayed on as a field worker and fundraiser until his death in St. Paul on March 1, 1921, at the age of seventy-six.

The MINNESOTA
CHILDRENS HOME FINDER
"In His Name"

PUBLISHED BY
THE CHILDREN'S HOME SOCIETY
OF MINNESOTA

VOL. XVIII No. 4   NOVEMBER 1918   QUARTERLY

GOODNESS IS THE ONE INVESTMENT THAT NEVER FAILS

2 *An equal chance*

The Reverend Samuel W. Dickinson "loved children and was kept young by being with them," board member B. H. Bowler wrote. During Dickinson's tenure legislation granting true kinship status made adoptions "legal."

The board of directors selected the Reverend Samuel W. Dickinson, "an able, high-minded Christian man" who had directed the Chicago district of the Illinois Children's Home and Aid Society, as the new administrator of Children's Home Society of Minnesota.

Dickinson, who began as superintendent in the society's twentieth year and served until 1927, introduced professional standards to its work and policies. He shared with many other progressive social workers of the period a concern for the future of the American family. There were more births among the poor, fewer among the more affluent. There were rising divorce rates, industrialism, commercialism, "a general hustle for money," and growing numbers of women and children in the work force. Dickinson thought society had a responsibility to act—through the work of organizations like Children's Home Society—when "the influence of the family is lacking."

Within days of his appointment in 1909, Dickinson represented the society at the White House Conference on Dependent Children. The conference, which stood as a high-water mark of child welfare thinking for years, established the principle that no child could be removed from a home solely for economic reasons. Dickinson was among those who favored temporary relief for the poor, pensions for mothers, and legislation requiring fathers to support children born out of wedlock. The conference also affirmed, Dickinson wrote later, the basic principle upon which Children's Home Society had been founded twenty years earlier—that "while the institutional orphanage plan had served a useful purpose, the natural and rightful place for the child was in the family home."

Dickinson advocated a professional approach to child welfare and supported the public health movement, concentrating his early efforts on improving and expanding the temporary care services Children's Home Society provided for dependent children and unwed mothers. In 1912, for example, he hired "a scientifically trained nurse," explaining that many of the children received at the nursery "were handicapped by some physical impediment or retarded in development."

In 1913 Dickinson decreed that no child was to be received without being carefully examined by a "reputable physician" and certified healthy and normal. The society relied on the volunteer services of several doctors until the next year when Dickinson hired Dr. W. D. Beadies of St. Paul. The kitchen of the Jean Martin Brown Receiving Home was remodeled, with a milk pasteurizer and large refrigerator added. Infants were weighed regularly on metric scales and systematic health records were carefully maintained.

That same year the St. Paul Baby Welfare Association appealed to the society to board infants at the receiving home. Although Dickinson gladly cooperated with the reformers, the society expected the situation to be temporary. The effect, however, was a more or less permanent increase in the total number of infants in the receiving home, which began again to look like an orphanage.

Perhaps because of the growing number of infants cared for by the society, Dickinson advocated efforts to reduce unplanned pregnancies. Most young unwed mothers, he believed, became pregnant out of ignorance. He suggested that public schools provide "sane and scientific" sex education. To serve the babies already born, the society began a long-running six-month nursemaid course to provide child care help both at its receiving home and for private families.

The primary work of Children's Home Society, however, remained "home finding," to which Dickinson also applied his scientific methods. "The casual observer does not realize the actual demand there always is for children for adoption," he wrote after retirement:

> The demand . . . is greater than the supply, but prospective parents are particular in choosing a life member in their home. No family wants a sick child, a child [who] is not bright and able to rank alongside other children in the community . . . The average child will meet these requirements, but it was found repeatedly that many children were not average: They were retarded in school work, were ill-mannered and queer.

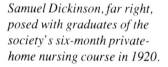

Samuel Dickinson, far right, posed with graduates of the society's six-month private-home nursing course in 1920.

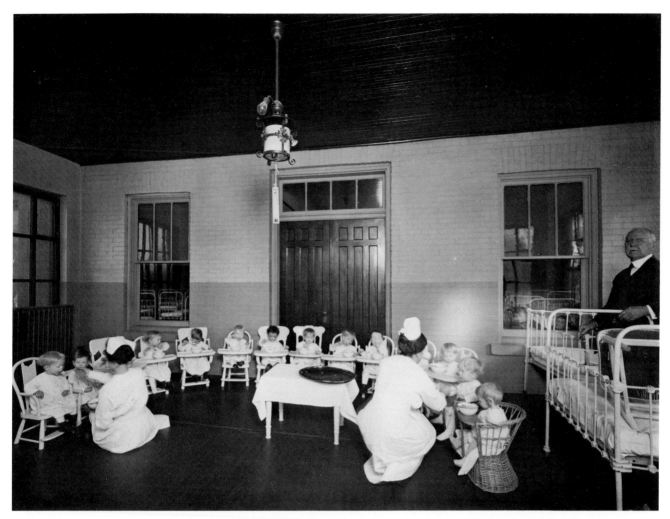

To learn why this was so, Dickinson authorized psychological testing. "If it was found a child was really mentally deficient, [he or she] must be returned to the county or sent to the [state] school at Faribault . . . diagnosed as unplaceable." The result of this standard, he wrote later, was that "of some 3,000 children [placed by the society and] examined in a survey . . . 99 percent of them were making good in the communities in which they lived."

By its twenty-fifth anniversary in 1914, the society had found homes for more than 3,600 children. As many as half the children, however, had been returned after the initial placement. Dickinson thought this indicated a need for greater deliberation at the beginning of the process. In contrast to the more informal approach of his predecessor, Dickinson instituted a rigorous investigation of prospective parents. "It requires courage to deny people who may be kind, who love children, but whose conditions of home life are not suitable," Dickinson reported to the board. He estimated that by 1916 the society rejected one-third of all applications by potential parents.

Dickinson approached child saving from a different direction than Savage, who had once remarked that the "true child saver" had a touch of the poet. Dickinson embodied the early twentieth-century ideal of "exact science" though he retained a human touch: On Christmas Eve 1916, reported *Children's Home Finder,* the children in the receiving home gathered round

Workers fed infants en masse during Dickinson's tenure. According to the August 1916 Home Finder, *one of the dishes served was "**Prunes:** Wash 1 cup of prunes, cover with cold water, letting them stand 6 to 7 hours, and place on stove, cooking in same water from 4 to 5 hours until very tender; then mash through fine sieve. To 2 tablespoonsful of mashed prunes add one level tablespoonful of moistened bread crumbs."*

Looking for Santa at Children's Home Society in the 1920s.

the tree to sing carols and open presents from Santa Claus, and Dickinson "read the account of the visit of the shepherds and the wise men to the Holy Child and offered prayer."

The White House Conference on Dependent Children that Dickinson attended in 1909 had been the catalyst for reforms in many states. Dickinson and his colleagues argued forcefully for child welfare reforms in Minnesota, and in 1917 the legislature passed thirty-five new laws based on the ideas that had emerged nearly a decade earlier. They regulated the work of agencies like the society through a system of inspection, visitation, supervision, and licensing under a centralized state agency called the Children's Bureau.

The new laws also made Minnesota the first state to confer true kinship status upon adopted children and modernized the process through which parental rights could be surrendered. Before 1917, any parent could go before a notary and sign a release relinquishing a child to the society's care. After 1917, only children declared dependent by a court could be committed to the society's guardianship. District superintendents of the society visited children who had been placed, even after adoption consents were issued, and reported their findings to the state.

In 1918, however, the society opened the doors of the receiving home to board children whose fathers were in the military service during World War I and whose mothers were working. Although the need ended with the armistice, the pattern of using the home as a more or less permanent residence did not.

The society's policy, Dickinson told the board in 1919, was to accept children "from three months to fifteen years . . . build them up physically, train them morally, and send them to school, and ultimately place them in good Christian homes where they will grow up to be useful citizens." This, he added, "is the work of saving boys and girls, some of whom might have become delinquent and gone to reform school."

Dickinson's insistence on the scientific approach continued. Caseworkers, for example, began an organized study of "temperament and mentality" by reviewing school records of the children in the receiving home. And the examination of every child by a physician now included tests for syphilis and tuberculosis. In addition, Children's Home Society began to enforce its rule that a child could not be placed with foreign-born adoptive parents unless English was spoken in the home.

Caseworkers began collecting as much "social data" as possible about every child received. "Wards want to know," Dickinson wrote, "about their parentage, their origin, their brothers and sisters . . . It is often a serious disappointment if we cannot give them these facts." He added: "Previous environment plays an important part in the treatment of children and should be known in treating psychopathic cases especially."

Like his predecessor, Dickinson maintained a high profile among his colleagues. He routinely presented papers to the annual convention of the

In addition to picturing babies awaiting placement, like this group in 1927, the Home Finder *offered advice to new parents. From the May 1923 issue: "Mothers do not realize that thumb sucking in babies is apt to produce enlarged tonsils, adenoids, indigestion and malformation of the jaw. Neither do they realize that pacifiers will do the same thing and are one of the biggest humbugs on the market. Our nurse says if the baby persists in the habit, make a splint from an ordinary starched cuff and clip it over the elbow. Baby can use his arm the same but cannot bend the arm to put the thumb into the mouth."*

These young residents of the receiving home benefited from Dickinson's scientific approach to child-rearing. As the May 1922 Children's Home Finder *advised, "Because a baby walks earlier and talks earlier than some others is no evidence that it is smarter . . . Because a baby laughs at the goody, goody baby talk is no intellectual evidence that it understands what is said. In fact, any baby can understand just good plain English far better than it can such baby nonsense that has no meaning and it would have to unlearn if it did. Because a baby likes candy, hot bread and coffee is no excuse for giving them to poison the system and ruin digestion."*

National Children's Home Society, and in 1923 he gave a talk about the society's work on national radio. "It was a unique experience," he wrote in *Children's Home Finder.* "Talking to an invisible audience of hundreds of thousands, from Maine to California, on the principles of child welfare as embodied in our work, was a great privilege."

One of the principles he espoused was children's rights. "Social workers everywhere believe today the dependent child is no longer to be considered an object of charity but as a member of society," Dickinson wrote:

> He has the rights and should have the privileges of any other child in the community. He should have education, affection, training and be given an equal chance in life. To secure this, the Children's Home Society places its wards with families of approved reputation, in good financial circumstances, of correct Sabbath observance who are temperate and have high ideals of character.

The society's use of some professionally trained staff and a scientific approach, Dickinson claimed, caused a "revolution . . . in the health and progress of children." Nevertheless, the society continued to rely a great deal on the work of volunteers and other untrained personnel. Ministers and church women—usually chosen for their good intentions and ability to raise money—continued to be the field workers. Investigations of prospective adoptive families often fell to local advisory boards, though the superintendent had sole responsibility for accepting and placing children. By 1921 the demand for infants was greater than that for older children, who were often taken on trips by field workers in the search for homes. Most case records were scanty, and for many children there were none at all.

Aware that changes were needed and reacting to the public's more critical attitude following the legal reforms of 1917, the society's board of directors asked the Child Welfare League of America in 1924 to make a study of its policies and practices. Although the board accepted the league's report— it recommended, among other things, more diligent casework—Dickinson made no effort to enact the recommendations, and dissatisfaction with the gap between standards and practices continued to grow.

Calling attention in 1925 to the number of Minnesota children who had families but who needed special care and physical treatment, Dickinson proposed enlarging the receiving home. His idea was to administer treatment to children with various physical problems, then return them to their own homes. Isabel Wilkinson, whose father James D. Humphrey was a longtime board member and benefactor, and her son James Humphrey Wilkinson agreed to build an addition next door to the receiving home, to be known as the Humphrey Memorial Building.

Ground was broken that summer, but soon after the clinic opened in February 1926, the society discovered—too late—that a new building was not enough. Funds for maintaining the new facility dried up. It turned out that existing hospitals performed the same services, often at less cost. The Humphrey Memorial Building was never used for its intended purpose.

That year the Child Welfare League of America conducted a study including not only Children's Home Society but all of the child caring and placing facilities in Minnesota. Its recommendations were similar to those of its study two years earlier. The society's board of directors accepted the league's report in October 1926 as a foundation for future policy.

At a May 1975 dinner recognizing his fifty years as a board member, George V. Thomson recalled Dickinson's custom of "addressing the board at every quarterly meeting, reporting that everything was going just fine." According to Thomson, however, a routine audit of the society's financial affairs in October 1927 disclosed that things were far from fine: "Our bonds, or most of them, were missing." An officer of the society's board, a well-known St. Paul businessman, had stolen negotiable securities worth $17,515—a large portion of the society's endowment. Although Dickinson was not involved in any way with the embezzlement, Thomson said the "Minneapolis Community Chest people warned that we might not get our allotment of funds unless we hired a more efficient person to head the staff."

Besides leading Children's Home Society of Minnesota for nearly twenty years, Dickinson had been elected president of the National Children's Home Society twice and had helped organize the Western Conference of Social Workers. But the board, reading between the lines of the league's 1926 report, signaled that the society was ready for a change, and Dickinson resigned.

Children's Home Society received many letters from grateful parents. The Home Finder *printed this one in 1916: "We like our little fellow very much; he is so affectionate and just a little bunch of sunshine. My husband is like all proud fathers and thinks we have the brightest boy he knows of."*

THE MINNESOTA
CHILDREN'S HOME FINDER

Published by
THE CHILDREN'S HOME SOCIETY OF MINNESOTA

VOL. XXXIII No. 1   FEBRUARY, 1934   QUARTERLY

Review of Society's Work in 1933

Population of Institution was at Maximum Several Times—Sixty-five Children Placed in Family Homes During Year—Happy Relations Maintained with Foster Parents

THE Children's Home Society of Minnesota had a busy year in 1933. More children were referred to it for care than for many years past, and its placements also exceeded those for many years past. The population of the Home several times reached the maximum of 50. That is the number of children the Society is licensed to care for in its institution. The license from the State Board of Control gives the Home authority to take care of thirty-two children over four years of age and eighteen under four years of age. Most of our friends probably know that the older children are cared for in the Jean Martin Brown building, erected in 1902 and still in excellent condition, while the younger children are cared for in the Humphrey Memorial building erected in 1926.

Eighty-five Children Admitted.

The Society was not able to give care to all the children referred to it in 1933, the total number of whom amounted to 176. We were able to admit during the year only 72 new children. Thirteen other children who had been previously placed out, but were for some reason given up by their foster parents, were returned to us. Altogether 85 children were admitted to the Home during the year. It is interesting to note the widespread distribution of our intake.

Came From Many Counties

The children who were admitted included in addition to those from Ramsey and Hennepin Counties, two from Lac Qui Parle County, one from Olmsted, one from Itasca, one from Fillmore, two from Crow Wing, one from Clay, two from Renville, seven from Goodhue, one from Ottertail, one from Morrison, one from Isanti, one from Kanabec, one from Freeborn, one from Wabasha, one from Mahnomen, and two from Anoka. While many of these children came singly, there were some fairly large family groups that came in together. Those from Goodhue County included one family of five children.

Placements Were Widely Distributed

Placements were distributed even more widely than our intake. We placed children in twenty-five counties including Ramsey and Hennepin. The placements were distributed countywise as follows: Jackson County, one; Anoka, three; Benton, one; Chisago, two; Goodhue, three; Wright, three; Kandiyohi, two; Mille Lacs, one; Pine, one; Itasca, two; Becker, one; Morrison, one; Nicollet, one; Nobles, two; Renville, one; Pennington, two; Ottertail, one; Cottonwood, one; Big Stone, one; Lake of the Woods, one; Isanti, one; Cass, one; Kittson, one.

Few Returns from Placements

The great majority of the children placed were, of course, infants, for the greatest demand for children is for infants. It is a notable fact which redounds to the credit of our very capable case supervisor, Miss Florence E. Johnson, that of all the children placed during 1933 only one baby was returned to the Home. Six other children placed during the year were returned, but four of these were children over twelve years of age. Such children are placed almost invariably without adoption in view. The placement of the older children during these years of the depression has been especially difficult. The record of only seven children returned out of 65 placements made during the year is one in which our Society takes a good deal of pride.

Health of Children Good

The health of our children was good on the whole throughout the year. We had very little sickness and we had no deaths among our children either in Home or those placed out. It has been our practice for some years past as soon as a child is taken down with a contagious disease, such as measles or scarlet fever, to have the child removed immediately to the hospital and thus prevent the spread of the disease among other children.

Recently we were consulted by a person making a study of an institution for children in another city, for the purpose of finding out to what extent our Home had been closed in recent years because of quarantine on account of sickness. The institution under study had been closed a considerable number of times during recent years, so that no children could go in or come out, because of the prevalence in the institution of communicable disease.

Continued on Page 4

WAITING FOR THE DOCTOR

Little Red Stocking

Returns Less This Year

Hard Times Cut Size of Gifts, But Many Old Friends Sent Money and Kind Messages

OUR good friend, the Little Red Stocking, did not do as much for our Society at Christmas, 1933, as in other years, but it still stood by us loyally. While we received only a little more than half as much as we received in 1930, yet we fell only about $170 behind what the stocking brought us in 1932. Considering the desperate hard times that we have been passing through the results from the stocking were very satisfactory.

This appeal has come to be expected at Christmas time by the friends of our work. Many of them would be greatly disappointed if they should not receive the stocking. Sometimes they expect it earlier than we send it out and write in to inquire about it. About ten days before Christmas a friend in St. Charles wrote us as follows:

Couldn't Wait for Stocking

"I haven't received the usual Christmas Red Stocking request for donation as yet for this year.

Continued on Page 2

Youth Wanders Far

Home Boy Tells Story

Runs Away From Foster Home and Has Hard Experiences in Southwest and on Pacific Coast

HALF doubting, we have heard and read for several years past stories of boys and young men who in great numbers have wandered over the country, riding on freight cars, begging their food, sleeping wherever they could. Many of us have been inclined to look upon these stories in the way that Mark Twain looked upon the premature story of his death—as greatly exaggerated. Now, however, the facts have been brought home to us here in a striking way by the experience of one of our own boys. Perhaps he would hardly be called a boy now, for he is in his twentieth year.

Gene Ran Away

Several years ago we placed Gene in the western part of the state. The placement gave him a chance to go to High School and we thought that he was of capacity that merited this opportunity. The placement went well for a time, but after about two years, for some reason that we have never been able satisfactorily to

Continued on Page 4

3 *To know the child*

Charles E. Dow's insistence on high professional standards made the society a widely respected child-placing agency.

Inspired by the recommendations of the Child Welfare League of America to establish modern practices conforming with accepted standards of professional child care, the society's board of directors hired Charles E. Dow to institute the new order.

Dow, who had been Connecticut commissioner of child welfare, made his intentions clear from the moment of his appointment in March 1927. He would make Children's Home Society of Minnesota:

> one of the best child-placing agencies in the United States . . . to which persons who want to adopt a child may turn with confidence that they will be fortunate in taking any child that the society may give them . . . [and] to which the courts may commit children in confidence that they will never be placed in any but good homes.

To signal the beginning of a new era of professionalism for the society, Dow immediately hired Florence E. Johnson to supervise the newly created Children's Service Department. A trained social worker, Johnson worked at Children's Home Society for nearly a quarter-century until her death in the summer of 1951. As a supervisor, she ended many traditional practices and insisted on professional casework methods, such as more selective intake practices, more thorough investigations, better follow-up after placement, and better record keeping. The changes protected both the child and the prospective family, in keeping with the policy of fitting each child to a good home. Johnson wrote in the August 1928 *Children's Home Finder:*

> The aim of the Children's Home Society of Minnesota is to know the child and to know the . . . home into which we place the child. Thus only can we give the child the greatest opportunity for self-expression and development, and give the . . . parents the companionship of a child who can measure up to their fondest expectation.

To signal a new era of professionalism, Dow hired Florence E. Johnson (second from right, in 1945) to supervise the Children's Service Department. Gathered with her are placement staff members (left to right) Alice Renard, Betty Miller, Valborg Kuefler, Mertice D. Walker, and (far right) Margaret H. Lighthall. But volunteers remained an important resource to the society. One group of women who began meeting at the Jean Martin Brown Receiving Home in 1933 mended more than 25,000 pairs of stockings in ten years.

The new order extended to the organization of the society. Dow quietly allowed the local advisory boards, which founder Edward P. Savage had established nearly forty years earlier, to fade out of existence. Though many of the boards had been inactive for several years, they represented the society's early, sentimental, and evangelical traditions. And, with Dow's recommendation, the society decided at the April 1928 annual meeting to affiliate with the Child Welfare League of America, an association setting professional standards and accrediting child welfare agencies.

One of Dow's most significant changes, however, was to return to Savage's fundamental idea—that the society should be only a temporary stopping point on a child's journey to a good and permanent home. Dow believed, announced a 1927 *Children's Home Finder*, that "the best place for any child who is normal physically and mentally is a good family home." Only in such a setting, the article declared, "can he have centered upon him the love and affection and care of . . . father and mother."

Under Dickinson's tenure, the Jean Martin Brown Receiving Home had, however unintentionally, become less a temporary residence and more a permanent boardinghouse. The Humphrey Memorial Building he championed had further focused the society on institutionalism though the building was never used as the residential clinic he intended. Under Dow's leadership, the society turned it into an additional temporary dormitory facility for both children and nursemaid trainees, and later into a nursery.

As such, the Humphrey Memorial Building served the new direction emphasizing legal adoption, as opposed to providing long-term care. The society would receive only normal children, keep them temporarily for care, observation, and training, then place them in carefully chosen adoptive homes. Children under age four were moved from the original Jean Martin Brown Receiving Home to the Humphrey Memorial Building. The society was licensed in 1927 to care for thirty-two children under age three and eighteen children over three. Less than ten years later, the proportions would be exactly reversed.

The society made an earnest effort to approximate family life in the receiving home. The children gathered frequently in the living room, and older children were trained "in the household arts, including bedmaking and dishwashing." They had their own well-equipped playground, chose their own clothing, and were free to invite friends to visit, even stay for dinner. The earlier emphasis on formal religious exercises declined, but each child was required to go to church and take a turn saying grace.

The Child Welfare League, completing its third study of Children's Home Society of Minnesota at the end of the depression year 1932, found "a homelike atmosphere" at the receiving home, but—anticipating the future—suggested "the society should keep its eye open to the possibility of using its buildings to better advantage or of dispensing with them entirely and of using boarding homes for shelter care." After all, the Children's Charter approved by the 1930 White House Conference had proclaimed:

> The rights of the child are the first rights of citizenship. For every child a home and the love and security which a home provides; and for that child who must receive foster care, the nearest substitute for his own home.

A keen issue of the 1920s and 1930s was: Should you tell your child he or she was adopted? The answer of Children's Home Society, stated frequently during this period, was an emphatic yes. The February 1928 issue of the *Home Finder*, for example, cited the experience of a woman who learned of her adoption at the age of eighteen:

> I lost confidence in myself and my heritage. I believed that all that was good about me was due to environment and all that was undesirable was due to my heritage, and I thought heritage far more important than environment. I lost faith in my . . . parents and my childhood friends as I believed they all had deceived me.

The financial problems that had dogged the organization since its beginning eased after the society joined the War Chest (forerunner of what was to become the United Way) in 1919. After the war, the society's operating money came from an endowment fund established earlier, payment for boarding, Community Chest grants from Minneapolis, St. Paul, and Duluth,

The society made every effort to approximate ordinary childhood experiences in its receiving home. So even the youngest children, here in 1927, got a chance to play in the sandbox and get some sun.

Right to the kitchen

As a teenager, Bobbie Hoffman (seated, far left), who was never legally adopted by her foster parents, enrolled in the society's nursemaid training program.

Bobbie Hoffman remembers when she arrived at the Jean Martin Brown Receiving Home with her two brothers and three sisters late one night in November 1935, after a long train ride from Omaha. "It was sister Betty's ninth birthday," she recalled over fifty years later. The youngest sibling—fifteen-month-old Rita (for her story, see page 53)—went to a foster home. "We older kids went right to the kitchen for hot chocolate and cookies, then up to the isolation room and bed." The next day, eleven-year-old Frank returned to Omaha.

The isolation room, on the third floor of the receiving home, was where all new children stayed for seven to ten days while they received shots and checkups. "There were toys aplenty—and books!" The children received all meals there. Matron Nellie Bloomenrader "came in at intervals to care for us. She also read to us—what a pleasure!"

After their period of isolation, Bobbie and her siblings Betty and Glenn joined the other children in the home. A younger sister went to the nursery next door. The front office was off limits, but otherwise the children moved freely about the home, under the watchful eyes of matron Bloomenrader and other workers. They awoke each morning at six, "threw back the bedding," then washed their faces and hands and brushed their teeth, dressed in clothes put out the night before, and performed chores. "Each was assigned little duties before breakfast—shake rugs, dust, clean baths, polish shoes, shake dust mops, help in the kitchen and dining room."

Once morning chores were done, the children assembled in the dining room. Someone was called on to say grace, they sat at assigned places, and the matron came around with "a jar of spoons and cod liver oil—we'd each get a teaspoonful." Breakfast was hot cereal, toast, milk, juice, and poached or boiled eggs—on Sundays, pancakes or fresh cinnamon rolls.

Some of the children cleared the breakfast dishes and reset the tables for lunch, while others washed and dried. Others were assigned to make beds and help get the younger children ready for school. After chores, the matron led them to the corner on their way to school. "We were often jeered at or made fun of being from the orphans' home."

"We'd return to the home for lunch—usually soup, sandwich, and fresh vegetables and fruit—then go back to school for the afternoon." After school, the children changed out of their school clothes, did their homework and afternoon chores. "We helped can, polish shoes, iron, and press"—and played. Sometimes "clubs would take us skating or to horse shows at the Hippodrome" on the state fairgrounds not far away.

They had a routine for dinner and evenings as well. The younger children were in bed by 7:30, the older ones by 8:30 or 9:00. "We said prayers together, kneeling at the side of the bed, led by the matron. Saturdays were for play and outings—after chores." Sunday, "always the best day," included Sunday School at the St. Anthony Park Congregational Church four blocks away and a big dinner at noon, play, and a light supper of sandwiches and graham crackers with chocolate frosting or yellow cake.

"Older girls and boys were given the privilege of folding the newsletter and the Little Red Stockings for mailing," Hoffman said. "We'd sit at the dining room tables. It was fun." At Christmas, a huge tree was set up in the living room and there were "presents, donations, and food galore. We'd go caroling and make cookies and decorate them."

Hoffman's saddest memories of childhood at the receiving home were the times when "adopters" came:

Miss Bloomenrader would call two or three children together and we'd get dressed in our Sunday best . . . We'd be taken to the front office . . . where there would be a couple. We'd stand in line in front of them with Florence Johnson present. We'd be asked our name, age, and other questions—what did we like to eat, what did we like to play—and maybe we'd be asked to sing. Then we'd go back upstairs to change our clothes. And we'd wonder which one of us would be leaving.

contributions from friends, and the Little Red Stocking appeal each Christmas. But the period of prosperity ended abruptly as the decade closed.

As the Great Depression settled in during the 1930s, income from all sources dwindled dramatically. The treasurer reported to the 1935 annual meeting that the society had closed the books on the year with a net balance of only $1.86. Contributions made up the society's entire income: Adoptive parents did not begin paying fees of any kind until years later—a fact the society pointed out from time to time during Dow's administration. "No fees, no contributions, no payments of any kind are required of persons who take children from Children's Home Society of Minnesota," the *Home Finder* reminded its readers in August 1937. Two years later, the society advised adoptive applicants that it would begin to charge a modest two-dollar filing fee:

> Few applicants for children probably realize the expense that is involved in making the investigation of their homes, calling upon their references, and if a child is placed with them, of making subsequent supervisory visits. These expenses include streetcar fares, meals when workers are away from home, a portion of the salary of workers while they are engaged in such investigation and rather surprisingly large amounts for postage and stationery and printed blanks.

And Dow reported to the board in January 1940 that:

> Our receipts from all sources other than individual contributions from directors and their friends are insufficient to carry on our work by the amount of nearly $150 a month. I do not see where any considerable saving could be made without a material reduction in either the quantity or the quality of our work.

In 1931, George V. Thomson, member of the society's board of directors, provided tools for a workshop. The boys built many things, but airplanes were their favorite.

The economy picked up with the onset of war in 1941, and the society's fortunes began to improve. War, however, imposed its own hardships on the society, mostly in the form of a widespread manpower shortage. "As far as our own situation is concerned," noted the *Home Finder* in May 1944, "it really is a womanpower shortage." Few cooks were available because women who in the past had done such work took "highly paid jobs in some war industry." The receiving home's laundress was pressed into service as breakfast cook, while neighbors helped out preparing other meals. Although the society added a staff psychologist "for studying children" in 1943 at an annual salary of $1,800, Dow reported the society's general salary structure

Children in the receiving home enjoyed varied social outings, including the picnic at right. The society encouraged their educations too. In 1936 a WPA music teacher instructed about twenty children in piano and singing twice each week.

was too low; many employees were leaving to work at jobs where they could earn more. By November 1945, the society had lost the services of both fund solicitors: One was ill and the other had resigned. "Can't find any to take their places," Dow reported.

During the early years of the Great Depression when the economic situation was deteriorating, the number of children at the receiving home had increased steadily. In normal times, the society had been able to place older children in free foster homes without difficulty—boys on farms, girls in the city. But the 1930s were not normal times, and as the availability of homes vanished, the average stay of older children at the receiving home increased from six months to a year. Dow described these older children as "too old to be petted, [but] too young to work."

The strong demand for younger children continued. Large numbers of young children, in fact, were coming to the society: Unmarried mothers and impoverished young couples, unable to care for their infants, were deciding on adoption for their children. Maternity hospitals, which had previously placed newborns themselves, now were referring them to agencies like Children's Home Society. The society soon discovered, however, that the economic status of many prospective adoptive parents had changed dramatically; now they were unable to meet basic standards.

"Please don't ask for little girls with large blue eyes and golden hair," Dow had written in the *Home Finder* in May 1927:

> There aren't enough to go around. Please don't all ask for babies. Some of the older children need homes, too. One of the happiest placements I ever made was of a girl six years old. Please don't all ask for girls. The boys must have their chance in the world, too. We have some that very much need a place in a good family. Please don't forget that it isn't always a question of adoption. We have some boys and girls who could be helped a lot by being given a free home in a good family. They could help the family a lot, too.

Between 1927 and 1937—the first ten years of Dow's tenure—the society cared for 912 children. About half were accepted for placement, the other half for temporary care. Of the 435 children placed in family homes during this period, 321 were placed for adoption, 114 for free foster care. Prospec-

tive adoptive parents favored girls over boys, younger children over older—
only twenty-five of the children placed for adoption were over five years
old. Twenty-five percent of all the children placed in 1937 were in foster
and not adoptive homes, an indication of their average older age.

The society's only real choice was difficult: to accept only young children, primarily infants, leaving older children to the care of the state. By the
end of World War II the need for the Jean Martin Brown building as a temporary receiving home had declined significantly, and the society leased it to
the Public Welfare Department in the summer of 1945 as a special treatment
facility for older emotionally disturbed children. The society retained the
Humphrey Memorial Building for the nursery and offices. Dow reported in
February 1946 that the organization was now able to "pour more of our income and more of our energy into finding homes for homeless children."
The previous year had been a record one for the society—107 placements,
all but one for adoption.

Independent adoptions—that is, adoptions arranged independently of ac-
credited placement agencies like Children's Home Society—were another
matter of concern to Dow. He reported in April 1946 that the 154 independent adoptions (of 1,012 total adoptions) in Minnesota during the year 1945
meant that "defenseless babies had the futures picked out for them by persons who are not competent to do so." Noting that child welfare laws had
developed over a long period "to do away with inhumanities to helpless children," Dow thought independent adoptions "dangerous" for several reasons.
There was nothing to prevent a mother, "probably under emotional strain,"
from changing her mind "after the foster parents have become fond of the
baby [but] before he is legally their child."

Another reason Dow opposed independent adoptions, he wrote in the
April 1946 *Home Finder*, was that in most cases the mother knew the iden-
tity of the adoptive parents. He cited cases that "resulted in tragedy" when,
years later, the birth mothers sought out grown children who had known
nothing of their existence. People arranging independent adoptions were
generally untrained and ill-equipped to do so, Dow maintained.

After the long winter of war and depression, it was time to take a fresh
look at society policies. The directors again asked the Child Welfare League
of America in 1946 to undertake a new study of Children's Home Society
of Minnesota. The league found that Dow's insistence on high professional
standards had made the society a widely respected child-placing agency and
recommended additional steps toward professional standards.

Social work, Dow noted in his final article in the February 1947
Children's Home Finder was "still largely an adventure in philanthropy"
when he joined the society in 1927. He had served twenty years as superintendent and helped the society celebrate its fiftieth anniversary (in 1939).
But he had reached the age of retirement and knew that a new leader should
preside over the approaching sixtieth celebration:

> A much younger man than I, one filled with the zeal and enthusiasm of youth,
> should be charged with the responsibility of pressing on toward these new goals
> and of bringing about the recommended changes.

Children's Home Society shifted its focus to infant care, leaving the state to provide foster care for older children. The receiving home was leased and later sold, and the Humphrey Memorial Building became both nursery and society headquarters.

THE MINNESOTA

Children's Home Finder

THE CHILDREN'S HOME SOCIETY OF MINNESOTA

FALL, 1951

4 *A suitable match*

Charles B. Olds, named executive secretary of Children's Home Society in 1947, turned attention toward modern thinking about child welfare.

In 1947 Children's Home Society turned to Charles B. Olds, director of the Maryland Public Welfare Department, for leadership. Born of missionary parents and reared in Japan—his work during the war was resettling West Coast Japanese-Americans—Olds had earned his bachelor's degree from Oberlin College and his master's from the respected University of Chicago School of Social Service Administration.

Determined to strengthen the society's professional standing established under Dow, the board of directors made it clear that Olds, known universally as Charlie, would have a free hand. The new executive secretary (the title was changed from superintendent shortly after Olds came to the society and later to executive director) expanded the staff, hiring trained social workers despite a nationwide shortage of such professionals. By 1952, the staff was bigger and more professional—almost every staff member had completed at least a year of graduate study in social work.

Olds first concentrated his attention on changing policies and practices to reflect more modern thinking about child welfare. The society's recent infants-only policy had overburdened the nursemaid trainees who cared for the children awaiting adoption. In addition, studies conducted by several states indicated that personal family attention was better for infants than group care in a big nursery like the one Children's Home Society operated in the Humphrey Memorial Building. So the society decided at the annual meeting of 1949, its sixtieth anniversary, to close the nursery, and Olds directed staff workers to place all children in temporary homes.

Nearly two decades later Olds told society members at another annual meeting:

> Today, even though the agency is serving more than three times as many children as in the days of the nursery, there are enough good families willing to give [foster] care to these children and every day proving that loving family care is essential for every child whether he [or she] be five years of age or three weeks of age. We have had some foster parents who have had more than 100 different babies in the course of several years.

This board of directors met for the society's annual meeting in 1948: (front row, left to right) Mrs. Robert Sullivan, Mrs. Paul Schilling, Mrs. Robert Ward, Mrs. Russell Bennett, Mrs. Valentine Wurtele, and Charles B. Olds; (middle row) George V. Thomson, Dr. H. S. Lippman, Lewis W. Child, Dr. Walter C. Coffey, and the Reverend George S. Siudy; (top row) J. Humphrey Wilkinson, the Reverend Glenn Lewis, B. H. Bowler, J. Russell Smith, and Dr. Arthur B. Hunt.

When Olds took on the directorship, common adoption agency practice limited placement to one child per family and barred families with biological children from placement at all. He reversed these policies. The society's fundamental role, Olds said later, was:

> to provide protection and security to children for whom it assumes responsibility. This means that the objective of the society is to find the right home for each child, rather than to find children for childless couples or others who apply for children.

So the society—and then other Minnesota adoption agencies—altered the focus and direction of adoption applications:

> Instead of putting . . . applicants through their paces, requiring them to meet certain rigid conditions, testing them and keeping them on the anxious seat, the agency accepts at face value the desire of the couple to have a child . . . The agency worker is not constantly looking for clues of pathology or for excuses for denying the desire of the applicants.

Although private meetings continued, the society lifted the curtain of secrecy and introduced group meetings to orient prospective adoptive families to the society and prepare them for parenting. This simple change showed prospective parents that they were not alone in wishing to adopt. Quickly realizing the significant benefits of group orientation, other child placement agencies followed the society's lead, extending the group approach to other services as well.

In the fall of 1954, the society paused to observe its sixty-fifth anniversary. Olds noted that Children's Home Society of Minnesota had since the early years of the century recognized the principle that "no child should be taken from parents simply because they are poor." The society's advocacy of this point, he declared, had helped establish the concepts of the Mother's Pension of earlier years and, later, Aid to Dependent Children. Olds pointed to other important contributions of the society as well. The long-running nursemaid program and its cooperation with other child welfare agencies, for example, had helped reduce the infant mortality rate in Minnesota from 70.1 deaths per thousand live births in 1915 to just 23.7 in 1953.

Anticipating the later direction of the society's services, Olds called for "more casework and some degree of financial help for the unmarried mothers who come to the agency." Not only were many of them young, with psychological problems, but they also struggled under "the crushing weight of the financial burden which falls upon them for medical care and maintenance during the latter part of their pregnancy." Fear of disclosure often prevented them from seeking public assistance or forced them to turn to the adoption black market for financial support.

The society had noted in 1947 the marked increase in out-of-wedlock births since the beginning of World War II. "A great majority of such children must be placed in adoption," Olds said, "largely because of the present harsh attitude of society in general toward the unmarried mother."

Olds and Children's Home Society became widely known for leadership on a broad range of issues affecting the welfare of children. He was selected executive secretary of the prestigious White House Conference on Children and Youth in 1950. "Inadequate family income, which deprives children of decent housing, sufficient food, clothing, medical care and other necessities of life, can profoundly impede the development of healthy personalities," he wrote. "One out of every two children living in large cities belongs to a family with less than a minimum standard of living." He advocated a national effort to construct low-cost housing, expand educational opportunities, abolish segregation, and improve hospital care and health services for children.

As in the past, the society asked the Child Welfare League of America in 1956 to examine its programs, policies, and procedures. Joseph Reid, executive director of the league, visited Children's Home Society in July and

These "boarding home mothers," who cared for babies awaiting adoption after the society's nursery closed, regularly returned with the babies for Clinic Day.

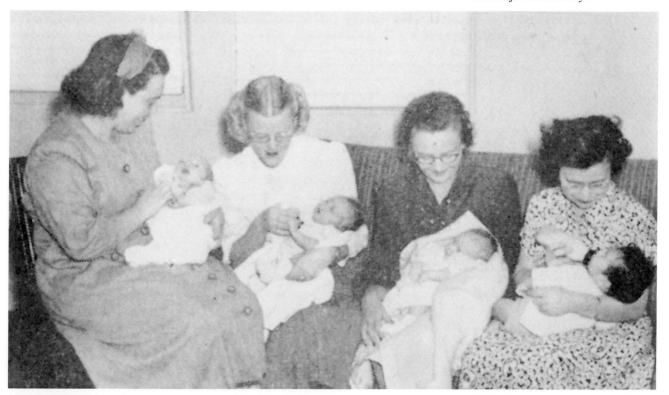

Adoption runs in the family

Mom and Dad already had David when they decided to adopt a baby girl through Children's Home Society in 1936. They waited three years before getting the call that all adoptive parents hope for. They had a choice of two girls, and they chose me. It was May 19, 1939, and I was four months old.

Five years later, they decided to adopt a second daughter, and Margaret became our little sister. She was four months old. I remember hurrying home from kindergarten to find Mother sitting in Grandpa's rocker with a small bundle in her arms. I tiptoed up, and she opened the blanket to show me a baby with legs, arms, and mouth all moving at once. My dolls didn't do that or look so soft.

With the adoption later of sixteen-month-old Mary, we became a family with three sisters and a brother. Adoption wasn't mentioned much as we grew up. We girls shared our fantasies: We were lost princesses from a beautiful kingdom or the daughters of a duchess and a duke with a stable and millions of acres. Sometimes other children teased us, but we knew Mother and Dad had chosen us especially for their own.

My husband, David, and I had been married nine years before we decided to adopt. It took me two days to make the first telephone call to Children's Home Society because I was so nervous. But as our social worker guided us through the adoption process, David and I learned things about ourselves we had never known before. Fourteen months after the call, we adopted two-week-old Sarah Elizabeth. Four years later Charlotte Anne joined our family.

I remember once when the two girls had spent all morning listening to their Grandmother Healey tell stories about David and his brother as little boys. Noticing their perplexed expressions, I asked what was wrong.

" Daddy is really weird," Sarah said.

"What do you mean?" I asked, surprised.

"Can you believe this, Mommy? Grandma said Daddy came out of her tummy—not from Children's Home Society!"

Growing up, Sarah and Elizabeth asked the questions that most adopted children ask: Who do I look like? Did my mother love me? But as they got older, the questions became more

Margaret, Charles, Mary, Sally, Elizabeth, and David Onan, above in 1952.

Sarah, David, Charlotte, and Sally Healey, above in 1981.

complex. I had recently read papers from my adoption file for the first time and felt comforted—I had roots somewhere, and now I decided it was time for our children to see their adoption files too.

Both jumped at the chance. Sarah read hers to herself. Charlotte stood and read hers aloud, proudly and confidently. Much discussion and discovery of each other's relatives and backgrounds followed.

Since that day, Sarah and Charlotte have talked often of their heritage. "No wonder I love horses—so did my birth mother!" "See this red highlight in my hair? It's from her."

Sarah, always the one to ask the most questions, was the first to say she would like to meet her birth mother. Both she and Charlotte, like many adopted children, feel the need to connect themselves with a real person. They hesitate because they're afraid of hurting me. They don't want me to think that they don't love me. But I know that they do.

—SALLY ONAN HEALEY
Board member, adopted person, and adoptive mother

recommended to the board's executive committee that it put more emphasis on minority placements, which were both expensive and time-consuming. Although the society already had a program for minority placements, Reid's challenge laid the groundwork for a statewide experimental project that Children's Home Society was instrumental in establishing in 1963.

Black children were at first not included in the minority project on the assumption, Olds admitted later, "that it would not be possible to place Negro children in Caucasian homes." Under pressure, the project was expanded to include black as well as Oriental and Indian children. "Transracial placement of Negro children," Olds maintained, however, "will not in all likelihood solve the problem of the need of Negro children for adoption in the near future . . . However, Minnesota and a few other communities throughout the nation are indicating that some of the children of Negro heritage can be integrated into the majority community."

Olds took a leading role in professional issues, too, presenting a paper at the 1964 National Conference for Social Welfare in Los Angeles recommending post-legal adoption counseling and other services. "We must assume that most adoptive parents and their children are having problems no different from those of any [other family, but] . . . adoptive parents are more likely to seek the help of child guidance clinics and social agencies in meeting their problems than parents of biological children." Urging child welfare agencies to establish services to answer post-legal adoption needs, Olds asked rhetorically: "Is it because of the fact of adoption that the parents are going to these clinics or is it because they are conscientious parents?"

The society also helped introduce the team method of social work. "Traditionally," *Children's Home Finder* explained in 1967, "the couple who comes to the adoption agency has been involved with one or at most two different case workers in the total process of home study, placement, and

At the urging of the Child Welfare League of America, Children's Home Society broadened its minority adoption program in the 1960s. Today the prevailing practice is to match black children with black adoptive families, while federal legislation dictates that American Indian children be matched with Indian families.

Social worker Margaret Steen with an adoptive family, about 1967.

post-placement service. Now, there is a team approach including several different members of the staff." The result was more complete and efficient service to adoptive families, as well as to other clients like unwed mothers.

Better service meant greater expense. When Olds became executive secretary, the society's budget was $42,000, and when he left it was $300,000. He credited the board of directors with foresight, courage, and hard work in raising the funds to introduce and operate expanded programs for children. Olds himself was one of the society's most effective fundraisers. According to board member George V. Thomson, at first Olds didn't believe the executive of a social agency like the society "should be handicapped by having to put much time on fundraising. But, being old enough to be his [Olds's] papa, I acted the part and set him straight. He got converted thoroughly and completely and became a good money raiser."

The society received money in 1947 from only three Community Chest drives—Minneapolis, St. Paul, and Duluth—but by 1967 it received such support from 270 communities in Minnesota. Individual contributions, especially from long-standing benefactors, continued to account for large portions of the society's income. The society receives annual income, for example, from the bequest of Earle Brown, who died in March 1963 after more than thirty years of service on the society's board of directors. His wife Gwen was also a director of the society (for nearly twenty-five years) until her death in 1947. Brown was the grandson of Captain John Martin, the Soo Railway and Minneapolis and St. Louis Railroad executive who funded the Jean Martin Brown Receiving Home in 1903. George Thomson recounted in a 1958 annual meeting address:

> Many a time I have gone to Earle and said, "Earle, we need so many thousands of dollars this year. I think I have enough people lined up for about half." And he would say, "All right, George, I'll be good for the balance."

Other significant financial support came from James Daniel Humphrey, his daughter Isabel Wilkinson, and her son James Humphrey Wilkinson (who had donated the money for the Humphrey Memorial Building in 1925). According to Thomson, Humphrey, a board member for twelve years before his death in 1923, "dearly loved little children and was vitally concerned with their welfare." He described Wilkinson as a person who insisted on "prudent management and proper conservation of the society's funds . . . [and as] one who parts with substantial cash when [the society] needs it."

Another family showing long and dedicated devotion to the society was that of the Whitneys. Alice Wheelock Whitney served on the board from 1931 to 1951, donating both time and money. J. Kimball Whitney, her grandson, followed her on the board in 1962. "I witnessed and participated in many changes during these years," Whitney recalled, "changes that brought growth and improved services to the organization." In adopting three children, he also benefited from the services of the society.

The constant need for greater funding was a common problem among child-placing agencies like Children's Home Society, primarily because they were forbidden by law to charge adoptive parents even for directly related costs. Despite the failure of earlier efforts to change the law, Olds took up the campaign anew. To those who thought fees the same as buying a baby, he responded: "When a couple has a baby born to them and pays the medical expenses, they are not buying a baby from the doctor or the hospital."

Such arguments by Olds and his colleagues persuaded the legislature in 1957 to allow child-placing agencies in Minnesota to charge adoption fees to a maximum of $300 (the ceiling has since been raised). The society established a sliding fee scale based on family income, waiving the fee altogether when it would impose financial hardship. Fees paid by adoptive parents help pay for services directly received, though the charges to this day have not covered even the majority of actual costs per placement.

By 1957 the society's need for money had increased in another way. Staff members still worked in the Humphrey Memorial Building, erected in 1925 for clinic, not office, space. Now, even its space was inadequate for the foster care and adoption services expanded under Olds. The conclusion was that only a new facility designed for the society's new needs would do.

One committee of the board began work on planning, another on raising the money to pay for a new building. A site was chosen just north of the receiving home—a corner of the same piece of property that Joseph Elsinger had donated in 1900. The planners at first envisioned a traditional rectangular building, but general contractors Myron Kehne and Associates suggested a trapezoidal building that would fit the odd-shaped lot. The cost was estimated at $200,000, but by the fall of 1958—even as the building was beginning to take shape—increases had pushed the total figure, including furnishings, to nearly $250,000.

Through pledges and gifts from hundreds of individual donors, however, the staff moved in to a paid-for building in 1959, just in time to celebrate the society's seventieth anniversary. There were offices and other working spaces for twelve caseworkers, the director, and clerical and other staff. The new building also contained a family room, a general meeting room, and a small clinic designed by the Mayo Clinic to serve infants awaiting placement. The second level contained ten more offices, left uncompleted for later expansion.

The dedication of the new building gave the society an opportunity not only to look ahead but also to look back. Banker D. Fay Case, one of the

The October 1961 Home Finder *reported "a copy of Dr. Spock's book is presented free to all adoptive parents at the time of placement if they haven't secured it already."*

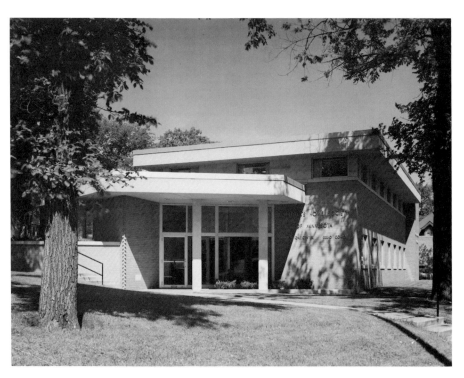

Ruth Schilling, president of the society's board, laid the cornerstone for the new adoption center (above right) at its dedication September 12, 1959. Sealed in the cornerstone were lists of staff, board members, and donors, as well as several issues of Children's Home Finder.

first children placed by E. P. Savage in the society's first year, 1889, was invited to the celebration. Ruth Schilling, president of the society, noted that more than 8,100 children had been placed in seventy years and that many more would find homes in the years to come—"children with handicaps, children of minority races, and children over the age of three years." Governor Orville L. Freeman said he was "especially pleased" that the society had expanded its services to seek homes for children over three years of age. "Giving the most intensive service to the less fortunate during childhood years can mean substantial savings both in public funds and human suffering," he noted, anticipating a widespread sentiment of the 1980s.

"As a long-range goal," the Child Welfare League recommended to the board in 1961, the society should become:

> a broader functioning agency by giving priority to, first, placing more of the "hard to place children" and, second, accept more unwed mothers for casework service. This expansion of service will require more fully trained mature workers . . . [and] more boarding homes skillfully selected for the older and harder to place children.

The Child Welfare League's Joseph Reid had made a second major recommendation to the society in 1956 concerning direct services to young mothers choosing adoption for their children. The board had not acted on the recommendation despite Olds's concern for the "rapid increase in the number of children born out of wedlock." The society had always assumed that the responsibility for preparing unmarried mothers for birth rested with public welfare agencies. A shortage of public monies, the time each case consumed, and the increasing number of cases, however, had conspired against effective counseling of unmarried mothers about the future of their children. That increasing numbers of unmarried girls and women were facing motherhood alone, with little or no counseling, was clear. Many did not have even basic biological information about prenatal concerns, delivery, or infant care.

Even more critical was the need for quality counseling about the parental responsibilities the young expectant mothers were about to assume.

The need for a temporary group home program for unwed mothers became increasingly evident, and—remembering Reid's recommendations of a decade earlier—the society began to plan a home and expand programs for unmarried young mothers, both before and after delivery. "Let us not be too hasty in concluding that this increase in the out-of-wedlock birth rate reflects a breakdown in morality," Olds cautioned as he concluded twenty years as the society's director. Citing a colleague who "maintains that our society is becoming more moral, not less," Olds noted that old standards of morality:

> required that a girl should marry, even at the point of a shotgun, the man who gave her a child out of wedlock. At best, such a marriage was unstable and provided an atmosphere of rejection and even hostility toward the unwanted child. The alternative at that time was shame and degradation for the mother. To be sure, there is some of this morality left today, but far less than before. We see fewer forced marriages and many more solo parents doing an adequate job of child-raising.

The year before Olds resigned to become assistant director of the Children's Aid Society of Oregon, Children's Home Society of Minnesota placed 333 children in adoptive homes. But in his parting message at the annual meeting of 1967, Olds predicted the number of children available for placement would probably begin to decline. Preparations for a small residential facility at 1887 Lincoln Avenue in St. Paul, the first of two group homes to assist unmarried mothers through the transition to single parenthood, were well under way as Olds stepped down. The society was on its way to becoming much more than an adoption agency.

Around the turn of the century, many home societies began using a red stocking as the symbol of need and giving during the holiday season. In 1909, little stockings of red paper were first sent to Minnesota children "to put in two cents for each year they are old." In 1926 the campaign was directed more towards adults, who sent money and clothing, toys, and other gifts to children in the receiving home. Like a gauge of the economics of each decade, the Little Red Stockings came back filled or almost empty. In 1948 the Little Red Stocking became the society's principal annual appeal, and it has since grown to become one of the major fundraising drives in Minnesota. Over the years volunteers have applied fundraising techniques such as the door-to-door approach, the use of celebrity appeal including that of actress Jane Russell, above, and display of the stocking, left, at the Minnesota State Fair. In the six years leading to Children's Home Society's centennial, the campaign has returned to mail solicitation, and the dollars given have increased steadily.

children's home news

summer 1974

5 *One life at a time*

Roger W. Toogood built a strong team of staff, board members, and volunteers to make Children's Home Society into a family of social services for children.

Roger W. Toogood, who became the sixth executive director on October 2, 1969—just three weeks after Children's Home Society of Minnesota celebrated its eightieth anniversary—took over in a time of crisis for the society and of profound change in the field of child welfare.

Following the resignation of Charles B. Olds, the board of directors had hired Harriet L. King, a native of Minneapolis and graduate of the University of Minnesota. She had served for six years as executive director of Nebraska Family and Child Services. "There will be no serious loss to the society to have a change in administrative leadership," Olds had written on resigning in March 1967. "A new executive can bring fresh thinking, stimulation and vigor to the agency." King, however, was in poor health and unable to meet the demanding schedule of her predecessor. Decisions previously made by the executive director were left to program directors and caseworkers. Coupled with a soaring number of requests for services and growing staff turnover, her frequent absences placed serious stress on workers, who King acknowledged in May 1968 were "pressured to the breaking point." Suffering injuries in an early 1968 automobile accident, she resigned after only eighteen months as executive director, recognizing "that the agency needs full-time leadership."

"It was a difficult time for the organization," Toogood recalled of his initiation at Children's Home Society three months later. "My whole approach was that we were starting off new and that we were going to work with one another." He established a low-key, first-name policy and set about building a strong team of staff, board members, and volunteers. Where King had been absent, he was everywhere—at staff meetings, board meetings, committee meetings, and professional conferences. He kept board members, staff members, and volunteers informed and opened lines of communication in both directions.

There was much work to be done for children. Times were changing, and in a more complex society, working with one child, one life at a time, meant abandoning some old ideas about homes and families and looking for more creative solutions. Half the poor in America, for instance, were children, Toogood learned at a meeting of member agencies of the Child Welfare League. The society, he noted on another occasion, had placed several children with single parents starting in 1967 and was one of the few agencies in the country accepting applications from single persons. In March 1968 the society had opened a group home for unwed mothers. And while many agencies were finding "changes in abortion laws resulted in significant drops in unmarried mothers in need of service," the society was seeing "expanded requests for services in all programs."

In response, the society reorganized its adoption program, which soon became the largest and most comprehensive in the United States. Undergoing a profound transformation, it reflected a basic change in attitudes that had begun in the mid-1960s. Many unmarried mothers, who previously might have chosen adoption for their children, now were choosing to be single parents. This directly affected the number of infants available for adoption, especially white babies. Waiting lists grew, and most agencies turned to other countries for adoptable children.

Recognizing in international adoptions the "opportunity to serve children who would perhaps not have adequate homes otherwise," the society had arranged its first adoptions from other countries in the 1950s. By summer 1955 it had found homes for more than six hundred infants through the "Baby from Abroad" program. At first, most of the children came from Germany; many were war orphans or children fathered by occupation troops.

The society arranged its first Korean adoption in 1967, and it has since been responsible for bringing more than six thousand children from South Korea to adoptive homes in Minnesota. The Seoul government began in the

Children's Home Society has the largest Korean adoption program in the United States. Since 1967 thousands of families have experienced joy like that of this couple when they met their new baby at the airport.

Alexander G. (Sandy) and Mary McLaughlin Hill first heard about Lee Song Ho, 11, from friends with children adopted from a Korean orphanage. Abandoned at an early age, Song Ho had been adopted in Korea, but his adoptive mother died when he was eight. According to Sandy Hill, the father's new wife wanted children "of her own," and life for Song Ho became one of riding the buses of Seoul to avoid her rejection.

The Hills decided to take on the special challenges that often come with adopting older children. Song Ho arrived in the Twin Cities on April 18, 1975, to become Peter Song Ho Hill.

Sandy describes Peter as a "survivor who has enriched the lives of many," including his adoptive mother, Mary, who died of cancer in 1979. After graduation from St. Paul's Macalester College in 1985 with a degree in Japanese studies, Peter rose quickly in management at Brooks Brothers Clothing, then moved to Japan in 1988 to teach and continue his studies.

"The experience of our family," wrote Sandy—now a board member—"is responsible for the adoption by close friends of six other children from Korea."

late 1980s gradually to curtail the number of Korean children allowed to be adopted abroad; Children's Home Society of Minnesota is one of the few agencies still helping American families adopt Korean children. (To deal with the numbers of children still in its orphanages, the South Korean government stepped up a program of in-country adoptions, pioneered by Hyun Sook Han before she joined the society's staff as a social worker in the fall of 1975.) The society now also finds adoptive homes for children from Central and South America, Hong Kong, India, and Greece.

While the adoption program expanded in new directions, Toogood's focus from the start was to establish a new agenda of services transcending traditional bounds. As director of the Child Welfare Division for Catholic Welfare Services in Minneapolis and earlier as a supervisor of Ramsey County's Child Welfare Services, he had seen the wide set of problems facing children and families. Asked to describe his vision by a board member interviewing him for the position of executive director, Toogood, an adoptive parent himself, replied:

Signaling a new direction for the society, Roger Toogood immediately upon appointment replaced the sign proclaiming the society's building an "Adoption Center" with the one at right.

Children's Home Society has a greater role than just being an adoption-focused agency. There are many other children's needs that we should also be facing. With your help, I want Children's Home Society to become the best child-focused agency in the country.

Though Olds had made important changes in services, the society's work still revolved around its eighty-year-old adoption program and there was no process for change. Toogood, a native of Rochester, Minnesota, who had received his undergraduate degree from the College of St. Thomas in St. Paul in 1956 and a master's degree from the University of Minnesota School of Social Work in 1958, knew that expanding services required planning. So in 1970, the society established a joint board-staff long-range planning committee headed by longtime board member J. Kimball Whitney, as well as an annual planning process for the entire staff.

"In every sphere of life, changes are occurring at a very rapid pace and they demand energetic response," Toogood wrote in a 1970 *Children's Home Finder* as he explored new directions. The earliest work of the long-range planning committee showed the need for quality day care, the board moved quickly, and the society opened its first day care center, in Roseville, in March 1972.

Since then, Children's Home Society has become the largest nonprofit provider of child care in Minnesota, with eight centers in the Twin Cities, two in Rochester, and one in St. Cloud. Operating in schools, community centers, low-income apartment complexes, and churches, the society offers day care for preschoolers at all locations, infant care at three—Cedar Riverside in Minneapolis, Dakota County Technical Institute in Rosemount, and St. Paul Technical Institute—and care through school age at Cedar Riverside and Highwood Hills. The Rochester, Cedar Riverside, and Spring Lake Park sites also provide services for children with special needs. All the society's centers provide parenting education, counseling, and health services.

In endorsing the Child Welfare League of America's day care standards to help children "develop as individuals who can enjoy and make their contribution to a democratic society," the society in its centennial year maintains staff/children ratios at each of its day care centers that meet or exceed state requirements. All staff workers are educated and experienced in child development, and the society maintains a variable fee structure that makes quality child care affordable to all.

The long-range planning committee had also identified post-legal adoption services as a priority. The society was already providing limited post-legal adoption services as the result of a proposal to Charles Olds in 1963 by staff member Marietta Spencer and two psychologists interested in older adopted children. Now Children's Home Society of Minnesota became the first agency in the country to organize post-legal adoption services formally and separate from other adoption services.

Children's Home Society and other child welfare agencies successfully lobbied the state legislature in 1977 and 1982 to extend laws regulating information exchange among the adoption triad—the adopted person, adoptive parents, and birth parents. This landmark legislation enabled the society to share non-identifying information previously unavailable. The comprehensive counseling programs, support groups, and public education materials developed by the staff established the society as an international leader in the field.

Three children enjoyed a snack at the society's Cedar Riverside Child Care Center in January 1985.

Another service area targeted by the first long-range planning committee dealt with a major social trend of the time—the rapidly growing rate of out-of-wedlock births among teenagers, even as the general birth rate for the population at large declined. The Minnesota Department of Health's Center for Health Statistics reported that more than 7 percent of the children delivered in the state in 1969 were born out of wedlock, many to teenage mothers. At the same time, the number of young single mothers deciding on adoption for their infant children was declining rapidly.

The society had provided limited counseling for unmarried pregnant girls for many years, expanding its direct services in 1968 with a maternity shelter for unmarried teenage girls at 1887 Lincoln Avenue in St. Paul. The idea of a temporary home for unwed mothers and their children went as far back as May 1894, when the board discussed such a residence to alleviate "the deplorable condition of many poor mothers who desired to keep their children but had no place to go."

The Summer 1983 Children's Home News *ran this photo of two Lincoln House West residents on the cover. In 1987 the residential treatment center was replaced by a program called Children's Home Young Parents, providing peer support groups and parenting education for adolescent mothers.*

In 1969 the society decided to turn the Lincoln House program from a maternity shelter to a residential treatment facility for high-risk teenage mothers and their children. By January 1972 transformation of Lincoln House was complete. During the next fifteen years, the house—a second opened in 1977 in Hopkins as Lincoln House West—served more than 360 young mothers and their children. While some women were older, most were teenagers between fourteen and nineteen years old, with children three years of age or younger. Most came to Lincoln House from the county court system because of abuse. Each young family lived in Lincoln House an average of nine months to a year, learning basic living and parenting skills. Most of the young mothers attended school or received vocational training.

The program became a model for similar facilities throughout the United States and Canada, but in 1982 government funding cuts forced the society to close the original Lincoln House in St. Paul. Lincoln House West continued to operate until the changing approach to social services forced its closing on July 31, 1987.

Call before your crisis becomes his. 641-1300.

Children's Home
Crisis Nurseries
of Saint Paul

A program of
Children's Home Society
of Minnesota.

*A public education campaign in
1985 used billboards and bus cards
to reach troubled parents.*

Still, an increase in reported cases of child abuse and neglect led to
another new service area for the society. In 1984, a twenty-six-agency community task force identified the need for a crisis nursery program for Ramsey, Dakota, and Washington counties and asked Children's Home Society to
provide it. The society's board and staff, already concerned about this issue,
responded immediately and enthusiastically. The society raised $275,000
in six months, exceeding its goal, and launched a new program called Children's Home Crisis Nurseries in the fall of 1985. "Each year one million
American children suffer from child abuse. More than 2,000 of these children die," the renamed *Children's Home News* reported: "In Minnesota during 1983 there were 11,422 reported cases of child abuse. Of these, 1,026
reported cases were from Ramsey County. An educated guess is that for every two cases reported, another case goes unreported."

A free service intended to prevent child abuse, Children's Home Crisis
Nurseries operate as private licensed shelter homes where parents may take a
child for up to seventy-two hours while they cope with personal crises such
as unemployment, abandonment, depression, and chemical dependency. The
society also provides crisis counseling, referral, and longer-term day care.

By the society's centennial—and Toogood's twentieth anniversary as
executive director—Children's Home Society offered thirteen different services including adoption and post-legal adoption, infant foster care and medical services, unplanned pregnancy counseling and teenage pregnancy prevention, child care, crisis nurseries, and parenting education programs.

The significant growth of staff and programs had led to serious over-
crowding at the society's headquarters in the 1970s. The unfinished spaces
left on the second floor when the building opened in 1959 had long since
been converted to offices, and still there was not enough room: The development department had to use temporary space nearly a mile away. In 1976 the
board authorized a two-story, $479,000 addition, and construction began
early the next year. Completed by the summer of 1978, it doubled the size of
the society's St. Paul headquarters.

By 1986, however, even the 1978 expansion was inadequate: Social workers doubled up in offices designed for one, threatening confidentiality in client meetings. When Park Bank, the next-door neighbor, announced plans to move across the street, the society paid $525,000 to buy and renovate the bank. The 7,200-square-foot expansion, however, relieved only the social workers from the crisis nurseries and some adoption workers who were able to move to private offices. The space shortage remained for other direct-service workers, preventing the addition of needed staff and the expansion of services in high demand. So the board authorized, in 1987, a $4.5 million Campaign for Children to acquire space, retire debt, and increase the society's endowment. Spurred by a gift from the William O. Naegele family, board members themselves contributed more than one million dollars.

The opportunity to increase space came less than a year later. Group Health owned a large building only seven blocks away, at 1605 Eustis Avenue. Constructed in 1929, the 17,200-square-foot facility had undergone two previous renovations as it served the Society for the Blind, then a Group Health mental health clinic. For a total of $1.2 million, the society acquired not only much-needed space for the present but also 3.2 acres of land to meet the needs of the future. Making room for direct services in the Como building, three of the society's four divisions and the executive director's office moved to the new building. The society approached its centennial with enough physical space to serve existing clients with existing programs and to accommodate new clients with new services.

Even with prudent management, the society has sometimes been forced to make hard choices—to turn away clients, limit or eliminate services, or turn away from new services. Despite the chronic lack of funds, Toogood from the beginning insisted on limiting government funding of programs to 30 percent of the total budget, fearing overdependence on public dollars.

The Children's Home Choir, pictured here in 1986, often performs at fundraising events.

Resolving the issues

At fifteen months, Meg Bale was the youngest of six siblings from Omaha, Nebraska, who arrived at the Jean Martin Brown Receiving Home in November 1935. While the others remained there, Meg went to a foster home; she returned to the receiving home late in January 1936 to rejoin her three-year-old sister in the nursery. There they stayed, apart from the older children, including sister Bobbie(see page 30), who recalled years later how she watched them play in the sunning room. Bobbie waved good-by when Meg and her sister left on October 26, 1936, to join an adoptive family.

Meg's adoptive parents lived for awhile in Coleraine on Minnesota's Iron Range. Then they moved to Duluth where the two sisters grew up. Meg didn't learn until 1961 that she had been born Rita and that, with five brothers and sisters, she had been removed from her birth mother's custody for neglect after the death of their birth father in 1935.

Meg's sister read a newspaper article in 1961 about a man named Frank Smith who was trying to find his brother and four sisters. Children's Home Society had helped him contact Bobbie. Together they tracked down Betty and Glenn. But Frank learned nothing about the two sisters who had been adopted together. They—Meg's sister knew—were the two siblings Frank was seeking. Meg learned, however, that her adoptive mother had not given the society permission to release information. Respecting her wishes, Meg chose not to make contact with her genetic family until 1975, after her adoptive mother's death.

Frank Smith's widely publicized quest for his birth family was one of a growing number of such cases, and Children's Home Society of Minnesota began to pioneer post-legal adoption services. Among its thousands of clients was Meg Bale. For Meg, resolving the issues of being "a member of two families—one genetic, one adopted, and both vitally important" meant telling her story, which she did in 1975 in post-legal adoption service workshops. In 1988 she wrote:

> I spoke about my experience of growing up in my adoptive family and of meeting my birth mother and siblings from a family I'd been a part of for the first one-and-a-half years of my life. I have always hoped I brought some insight to the people

Meg Bale, left, with Glenn, Bobbie, Frank, and their birth mother.

> in these workshops, but whether I did or not I certainly know that speaking about my experience was an important part of my personal journey.

Joining the post-legal adoption staff in 1981, she said, "felt right because Children's Home Society holds a very special place in my heart as a bond to my history, which directs me into my future." Her own experiences guide her in offering help to others facing the complex feelings and sensitivities of similar contacts:

> Helping clients to recognize, appreciate, and resolve these complexities is fascinating and at times exhilarating—and sometimes frustrating. Reaching out to clients on behalf of other clients, be it a birth parent, birth daughter, birth son, or a sibling—starts a process that can be scary and confusing as well as exciting. To be able to guide and support them through an experience that most people never have is also a tremendous responsibility and a unique privilege.

Children's Home Society holds several annual events, two of which have a long history. One is the annual picnic, which began some time during the 1920s. Children's Home Finder *first mentioned it in August 1929: "Perfect weather and good chance to go swimming [at Turtle Lake]—everybody from three years up had a good time." By 1946, the event had been taken over by the Associated Parents group. The Associated Parents, active until the 1970s, also sponsored the other long-running annual event, April Showers (above in 1985). "For the benefit of the babies in our nursery," those attending the first April Showers in 1946 brought some seventy packages of "quilted pads, gowns, shirts, stockings, booties, dresses, diapers, bottles and nipples, sheets, blankets, and toys." The 1961 April Showers was held in the evening, complete with dance music: "Those who desire to 'twist' may do so at their own risk," advised the* Home Finder.

Some questioned his policy during the years when federal money was readily available for a variety of social services, but the wisdom of his position became clear when funding of such services declined.

The question of funding went to the heart of a central issue of the 1970s and 1980s—government involvement in social welfare. Contributions from the United Way—the largest single source of nongovernment funding for voluntary agencies, according to the Child Welfare League of America—declined steadily from a high of 23.6 percent in 1960 to a low of 9.1 percent in 1980. The Reagan administration cut federal spending for social services on the theory that the voluntary sector would step in, but Toogood in 1988 cited the statistics of the Child Welfare League above, noting that:

> We are paying the price for cuts in federal spending for social services. What we've let happen is a dramatic decrease in funds and programs for housing, food, and services in general. Children are paying the consequences. The whole nation is struggling today because children have not been a priority. What I've been trying to do as head of Children's Home Society for the past twenty years is to make children's needs our top priority.

At the same time, Toogood believed voluntary private agencies like Children's Home Society have the potential to provide needed human services more effectively than government, and at less cost. "At a time when some private agencies were cutting back and many were not growing, we set about trying to do more," Toogood said. "We took an aggressive leadership role to identify the top community needs and raise the money for services to meet them."

And so Children's Home Society has relied increasingly on contributions from individuals. To raise such funds, the society combined public relations and financial development into a single department—Communications and Development. And while many comparable agencies might be delighted with one dollar contributed for every ten dollars in the budget, Children's Home Society could count three contributed dollars, with the cost of fundraising held to 5 percent of total income.

Children's Home Society of Minnesota has endured for a century as a leading provider of child welfare services in large measure because of the strengths of its executives. Time distills the unique contributions of each, but under Toogood's leadership, the board and staff of the society have significantly broadened services, initiated much-needed long-range planning, and applied prudent management techniques.

While all these have strengthened, through Children's Home Society, the children and families it serves, a strong voice of concern may be Toogood's most important contribution. In the tradition of the society's founder, Toogood has played an active role in a wide variety of professional associations, including the national advisory board of the Child Welfare League, the Minnesota Corrections Authority Advisory Commission, and the Advisory Committee of the North American Center on Adoption. Through such involvement he has influenced state and national legislation on issues including child-abuse reporting, adoption, and foster care.

Twenty years after Toogood promised the board of directors that Children's Home Society would "become the best child-focused agency in the country," few people in a position to know would doubt it has done so.

For friends like these, said Roger Toogood in 1988: "We must continue our work as a child-focused agency, broadening our family services to enable families to do a better job in rearing their children. We must be stronger advocates for all children."

With characteristic modesty, Toogood said:

> All we know is what we hear from the Child Welfare League of America and others who follow what is going on around the country—but I think we're certainly *one* of the best. Whatever we've achieved has been the result of a dedicated team effort by staff, board, volunteers, and donors.

Edward P. Savage set out in 1889 to save the children he saw growing up in squalor, neglect, and abuse. He believed child saving was everyone's responsibility, and for a hundred years the society he founded has often quoted him: "There is a need for a good family for every child—and woe to me if I do not help make it possible."

As the society prepared to observe its centennial, a cynic might have recited appalling statistics reflecting conditions facing children today and asked what difference the society has made. Even Roger Toogood faced the future with deep concern. "Family members are not supporting one another as they used to," he noted. "In today's value system, respect and honesty no longer seem so important. I see much more violence today and much less caring for others—for the poor, the elderly, and the young." But the cynic's statistics and the society's concerns are the strongest arguments for the continued vitality of Children's Home Society of Minnesota. "Our services in the future will revolve around supporting the family. The decreasing number of children in America means that every child becomes even more important." If the crisis facing children is greater today than ever, then our responsibility is at least the same as Savage's: To save the children and to give them good homes—one child, one home, one life at a time.

Members of the board

Waldo E. Hardell*	1948-82	Mrs. Hubert Kuefler (cont.)	1970-76	George S. Nolt	1889-89
Mrs. Reuel D. Harmon	1939-43	W. F. Kunze	1929-34	Dr. Cyrus Northrop*	1889-95
Dr. Dale B. Harris	1954-58	Mrs. Earle F. Kyle	1956-58	Mrs. John Northrop (Darlene)	1974-79
Mrs. J. Arthur Harris	1943-47	N. H. Laird	1891-91	M. J. Norton	1895-11
Hugh Harrison*	1889-97	William P. Laird*	1966-	The Rev. E. M. Noyes	1890-08
Dr. Percy W. Harrison	1945-59	James R. Landy	1942-44	Carole A. Olson	1981-
S. C. Haskell	1903-11	Mrs. Victor E. Lapakko	1963-64	David T. Olson	1978-83
The Rev. C. E. Haupt	1915-42	Frank W. Lauderdale	1909-13	Everett T. Olson	1958-63
Dr. Winfield S. Haycock	1953-58	L. W. Leach	1920-36	C. W. Onan	1944-56
James Hazen	1963-68	Henry Lee	1973-74	W. J. Oppenheimer	1928-30
Sally O. Healey (Mrs. David)	1976-	Myong C. Lee	1975-77	Chas. E. Otis	1891-91
The Rev. Heath	1892-94	Mrs. Ronald Lee	1974-79	Mrs. Ted Ottinger	1952-59
John W. Hedback	1964-75	Robert Letson	1970-74	The Rev. C. N. Pace	1923-27
Coleridge T. Hendon	1972-81	The Rev. Glenn F. Lewis	1946-53	Rodney F. Paine	1933-61
C. E. Hendrick	1920-22	Dr. H. S. Lippman*	1932-44	W. S. Pattee	1907-11
Sandra L. Hesse			1947-60	Jeno F. Paulucci	1960-79
(Mrs. Robert Poor)	1974-88	Mrs. Elmer J. Lindquist (Alice)	1961-	O. E. Peltola	1955-56
Mrs. C. G. Higbee	1896-01	Mrs. James R. Little	1962-63	Mrs. Lee R. Pemberton	1956-78
Alexander G. Hill	1986-	Mrs. J. C. Litzenberg	1936-38	Mrs. George T. Pennock (Jevne)	1967-
Louis W. Hill	1932-38	The Rev. Benj. Longley	1898-03	Douglass E. Perkins, M.D.	1963-
The Rev. G. H. Hills	1906-08	Charles H. Loomis	1958-80	James R. Peterson	1971-74
Francine M. Hitchcock	1983-	Dr. Arnold Lowe	1957-66	Mary Ellen Peterson	1979-
Timothy Hitchcock	1977-79	The Rev. E. G. Lund	1904-05	Mrs. Orville Peterson (Elizabeth)	1965-75
The Rev. J. C. Hoblitt	1891-02	Loren B. Lund	1960-81	Mrs. Perry Peterson	1961-63
Mrs. P. J. Hoffstrom	1950-54	F. W. Lyman	1903-06	The Rev. C. J. Petri	1896-02
F. A. Holman	1892-95	Mrs. Frederick C. Lyman (Clara)	1931-47	J. O. Pierce	1905-07
Mrs. Ralph Holmberg (Corinne)	1967-86	Miss Kathleen Lyons	1940-40	Frank B. Platt	1912-16
Mrs. P. R. Holmes	1920-29	The Rev. H. C. Mabie	1889-90	Donald Plowman	1961-67
Karen H. Hubbard	1983-88	James MacRae	1957-65	Richard G. Plufka*	1974-
O. M. Huestis	1917-19	The Rev. E. E. Madeira	1906-09	Mrs. William H. Plummer	1950-61
The Rev. C. A. Hultkranz	1903-16	Mrs. Geo. A. Mairs	1923-30	R. Trevor Pollock	1962-63
J. D. Humphrey	1911-22	Mrs. Samuel Mairs	1934-38	Mrs. John W. Poor (Lucy)	1951-56
Dr. Arthur B. Hunt	1945-67	Mrs. Hal Mallon	1957-57	George C. Power Jr.	1987-
C. J. Hunt	1908-10	Mrs. Harold S. Marks	1952-58	Henry G. Ramme	1959-62
The Rev. Pleasant Hunter*	1895-99	The Rev. Frank C. Martick	1960-69	Renee Ransom	1984-
Mrs. James G. Huntting (Laura)	1959-	Mrs. Milton D. Mason	1946-54	Mrs. Paul D. Redleaf (Rhoda)	1975-
Mrs. Ward Huntzinger	1953-62	Mrs. William McAllester	1974-81	James Reeves Jr.	1965-72
Dorothy A. Hyde	1985-	Mrs. C. Naumann McCloud	1919-31	Sydney Rice (Mrs. Robert J.)	1969-80
The Rev. Ingersoll	1895-97	Frank McCray	1985-	C. Donald Rieck	1958-62
Bill Ingram	1955-60	Mrs. A. R. McGill	1913-31	The Rev. W. B. Riley	1909-10
Mrs. Archibald B. Jackson	1938-39	The Rev. Alex McGregor	1900-08	August Rivera	1981-86
Alex Leslie Janes Jr.	1954-87	Carolyn McKay, M.D.	1976-85	Edward H. Roberts	1918-21
Albert C. Jerome	1921-50	The Rev. McKinley	1895-97	J. K. Robinson	1915-26
	1953-61	Dr. Jeanette McLaren	1921-25	Richard A. Rohleder	1964-76
Duane Johnson	1972-76	Dr. Geo. E. Merrill	1894-97	Mrs. Hamilton Ross (Sally)	1955-66
The Rev. E. Johnson	1904-13	Scott Meyer	1981-	Mrs. E. A. Russell	1895-12
Kathleen Johnsen (Mrs. Arvid)	1985-	Betty Lou Meyers	1976-80	The Rev. A. W. Ryan	1916-23
The Rev. L. P. Johnson	1903-04	Ken Middlebrooks	1988-	Judge Gaylord A. Saetre	1960-68
Matthew U. Johnson	1983-87	Mortimer Miley	1957-69	Mrs. J. R. Sandve (Wanyce)	1954-
Trudy Johnson	1984-	Mrs. Sherman H. Miller (Carol)	1978-79	Hugh K. Schilling	1986-
Mrs. Harrison R. Johnston	1932-38	William D. Miller	1979-81	Mrs. Hugh Schilling (Peggy)	1980-86
Mrs. Robert H. Johnston	1928-31	W. B. Mitchell	1920-30	Mrs. Paul A. Schilling (Ruth)*	1943-
William F. Jones	1986-	Gerald Moore	1950-50	Harvey J. Schneider*	1958-
The Rev. W. H. Jordan	1911-27	The Rev. E. N. Morgan	1895-95	Mrs. Carl T. Schuneman	1930-35
Dr. Gordon R. Kamman	1938-51	John W. Morrison	1957-60	Mrs. Lyndell Scott	1957-59
The Rev. John C. Kauffman	1964-69		1966-78	The Rev. Theo. Sedgwick	1903-09
Dr. Roger D. Kempers	1967-88		1986-	Mrs. Kenneth Seeley	1947-49
Mrs. C. S. Kennedy	1936-41	Frank E. Morse	1937-42	Nobel Shadduck	1942-43
O. W. Kerr	1907-16	Mrs. Karl Moser	1967-74	C. K. Sharood	1909-12
J. N. Kildahl	1915-21	Miss Jessie A. Mulvey	1931-49	The Rev. E.W. Shurtluff	1899-05
Charles F. King	1952-62	Hollis R. Murdock	1891-91	The Rev. George S. Siudy	1948-53
Mrs. Charles King	1972-74	Albreta Murray	1987-	The Rev. S. A. Skogberg	1896-96
E. B. Kirk	1908-47	Mrs. John Musser	1951-56	Albee Smith	1889-98
Chas. Kittleson	1891-24	Mrs. Paul N. Myers	1928-49	Edward M. Smith*	1959-74
The Rev. K. Koch	1907-28	William O. Naegele*	1972-	John Day Smith	1904-10
Dr. C. R. Kollofski	1958-60	A. E. Nelson	1910-27	The Rev. Joseph E. Smith	1889-91
The Rev. J. A. Krantz	1916-26	Floyd Nelson*	1949-67	J. Russell Smith	1927-58
Claude G. Krause	1933-39	Mr. Nichols	1893-94	Mrs. H. S. Sommers	1916-22
Marshall Kriesel	1973-80	H. P. Nichols	1896-97	The Rev. Geo. Soper	1898-99
Mrs. Hubert Kuefler (Valborg)	1962-68	Dr. Willemina Niosi	1974-80	Robert S. Spong	1988-

Index

Staff *

Kelly Alfaro
Doreen Amy
Carol Anderson
Tracy Anderson
Victoria Anderson
Elizabeth Apold
Julie Archbold
Joyce C. Arnes
Pamela Arnold
Amin Babvani
Margaret Bale
Teri Bell
Laurel Bennett
Lon Berg
Marlene Berglin
Allan Block
Audrey Bogen
Sheryl Breitman
Diane Bremseth
Mary Brendel
Carol Brennan
Julie Brovold
Linda Brovold
Barbara Brown
Kristen Brown
Vicky Brown
Debra Brua
Catherine Bruening
Judy Burns
Brenda Campbell
William Cappel
Flo Carlson
Laura Carlson
Monica Carlson
Claire Chase
Alice Chatham
Debbie Cheney
Mary Chesemore
Pamela Chlebeck
Lynnette Christiansen
Robert Cincotta
Agnes Ciolkosz
Linda Claxton, MSW, ACSW, CSW
Tammy Coller
Elizabeth Collinge
Michael Collins
S. April Conlee
Deborah Contag
Cynthia Countz
Barbara Bear Crandall
Adriane Dabrowski
Sandra Daley
Leola Daul
Judy Davis
Melissa DeWolfe
Doris Dean
Jill Disrud
Mae Belle Doty
Kristine Douglas
Therese Downey
Mary Du Chaine
Sherrie Eggert
Fawkia El Masry
Susan Elliott

Lori Estvold
Lillian Evenson
Jo Ann Falkowski
Carmen Ferderber
Jean Flakey
Gina Frank
Kelly Franzen
Debbie Freyberger
Mary Fulton
Mavis Gaul
Verlene Gaul
Stephen Gerber, MSW, MA
Kandace Gerding
Nona German
Ericka Golden
Jane Grant
Diane Gusek
Corinne Hadler
Judith Haines
Hyun Sook Han
Renaye Harn
Carol Harper
Vicki Hayes
Nancy Haynes
Yvette Hazen
Lynn Heibel
Julie Hermes
Gloria Hesly
Lynne Hessler
Barbara Heyn
Sharon Holten
Gina Honkala
Carolyn Hoolahan, MSW
Jayne Hopkins
Carol Houlton
Ann Huber
Michelle Hueg
Vina Hueg
Marilyn Igel
Beverly L. Jacobson, MSW
Zebune Jayatilaka
Mira Jejurikar
Cindy Jenco
Denise Jennrich
Debra Jensen
Angela Johnson
Christine Jones
Kamau Kambui
Laura Kary
Dianne Kelly
Karen Kilduff
Eileen Kimitch
Elaine Kirchoff
Sue Kjome
Susan Knowles
Linda Knudson
Sharon Kramlinger
Kristine Kroll
Usha Kumar
Arlyne La Forge
Sandra Landberg
Sonia Larson
Judith Lee
Linda Lehman
Diane Brady Leighton, MSW

Angela Lien
Elizabeth Lillevold
Tammy Limpert
Suzanne Lodmill
Evelyn Lovaas, MA, CAE
Katharine Lovelace
Sharon Lovgren
Diane Lowry-Luther
Carolyn Lund
Mary Anne Maiser, MA
Catherine Maniaci
Barb Mathias
Elizabeth Maunu
Barbara McGuire, M.Ed
Michelle McNeese
Terri McNeil
Maura McNellis-Kubat
Melba Meier
Marjorie Mereen, MSW, ACSW
Margaret Merriman
Diane S. Miller, MSW, ACSW
Dolores Miller
Evelyn Mitchell
Kathy Mitchell
Jeffrey Mondloh, MSW, ACSW
Elaine Morgan
Susanna Morris
Jean Muckelroy
Cindy Myroniuk
Shirley Nellen
Linda Nelms
Roxanne Nelson
Sandra Nelson
Jeanne Neuenfeldt
Denise Nikkola
Kim Nissen
Mary Ann Nord
Joyce Norgard
John O'Brien
Kathleen O'Sullivan, MS
Kathryn Oftelie
Jacqueline Olafson
Mary Olesen-Rettinger, MS, MFT
Machell Oliveraz
Eunice Olson
Kimberly Osborn
Stephanie Oskie
Joan Overkamp
Diane Oxtra
Larry Parrett
Jean Perkins, MSW, ACSW
Barbara Perpich
Kaye Perry
Deanne Peterson
Joanne Peterson
David Pilgrim, MA
Julianne M. Prow
Kimberly Radke
Jean Ramsay, MA
Karen Redman
Debra Reynolds
George Richardson
Susan Rickers
Sandra Rieder
Kathleen Robinson

Elena Rodriguez
Laurene Roller
Linda Ronning
Lana Rozell
Judith Russell
Marion Saiko
Teresa Sandberg
Rita Sanderson
Jean Sargent
Mary Scanlan
Elaine Schmidt
Henry Schoonover
Cathy Shapiro
Patricia Shepherd, MA
Linda Shores
Beverly Simmons
Michael Smith
Sharon Smith
Lisa Smuda
Marietta Spencer, MSW, ACSW, CSW
Theodore Stamos, MSW, ACSW
Pamela Stephens
Kathleen Stoick
Christiana Laederach Stolpestad
Harold Strait
Shirley Strebbing
Margaret Studaker
Karen Svendsen
Teresa Swenson
Joan Szymanski
Jill Tesch
Teri Thomas
Nicole Thompson
Angela Tomaino
Karen Tomczak
Roger W. Toogood, MSW, ACSW
Marian Trautmann, MS
Ana G. Trejo
Lisa Van Alstine
Ruth Van Ness
Vickie Van Ness
Kathy Van Riper
Sandy Voves
Kathy Voyda
Carrie Waldock
Nancy Waldock
Kim Waldron
Maxine Walton, MS
Sandra Wesolowski
June T. Wheeler, RN, PHN
Mary Whitney
Zoe Ann Wignall
Marie Wikstrand
Lisa Willey
Allyson Williams
Karla A. Williams, CFRE
Lyla Willingham
Leilani Wilson
Karen Wolf
Megan Wollner
Mary Beth Woods
Sylvia Yarney
Lori Ann Zimmel

*January 1989, Children's Home Society of Minnesota